THINK ABOUT SCHOOL?

Research into the factors associated with positive and negative attitudes towards school and education

A Report for the National Commission on Education

K
3
KEY

Wendy Keys and Cres Fernandes

Published in 1993
by the National Foundation for Educational Research,
The Mere, Upton Park, Slough, Berkshire SL1 2DQ

ISBN 0 7005 1333 7

CONTENTS

ACKNOWLEDGEMENTS   (i)

FOREWORD   (iii)

PART I:
AN INVESTIGATION OF THE MOTIVATION TOWARDS SCHOOL
AND LEARNING OF SECONDARY SCHOOL STUDENTS

CHAPTER 1: INTRODUCTION   I-3

1.1   The background to the study   I-3
1.2   The structure of Part I of the report   I-4

CHAPTER 2: THE DESIGN AND ADMINISTRATION
OF THE STUDY   I-5

2.1   The design of the research   I-5
2.2   The content of the questionnaires   I-5
2.3   Sampling, administration and response rates   I-7

CHAPTER 3: THE STUDENTS AND THE SCHOOLS   I-8

3.1   Introduction   I-8
3.2   Catchment area and intake information provided by the schools   I-9
3.3   Information on examination results provided by the schools   I-11
3.4   Information on consultation, reviewing and reporting
procedures provided by the schools   I-13
3.5   Background information provided by the students   I-15
3.6   Summary   I-17

CHAPTER 4: A COMPARISON OF THE RESPONSES
OF YEAR 7 AND YEAR 9 STUDENTS   I-18

4.1   Introduction   I-18
4.2   Attitudes towards school and learning   I-19
4.3   Teachers, teaching and the maintenance of discipline   I-28
4.4   Students' behaviour in school and out-of-school activities   I-35
4.5   Parents' attitudes to school and education   I-43
4.6   Summary   I-48

CHAPTER 5: FACTORS ASSOCIATED WITH MOTIVATION
TOWARDS SCHOOL AND LEARNING   I-52

5.1   Introduction   I-52
5.2   The selection of an outcome measure   I-52
5.3   The input measures   I-54
5.4   The results of the correlation and regression analyses   I-54
5.5   Summary   I-59

CHAPTER 6: OVERVIEW AND CONCLUSIONS   I-61

6.1   Introduction   I-61
6.2   Comparisons between the levels of motivation towards
       school and learning of students in Year 7 and Year 9   I-62
6.3   The factors associated with motivation towards school and learning   I-63
6.4   Other important findings of the research   I-64
6.5   The main implications of the research   I-65

APPENDICES   I-69

Appendix 1: National Commission on Education   I-69

Appendix 2: The development of the scales and other measures for
             inclusion in the correlation and regression analyses   I-71

Appendix 3: Factors associated with motivation towards school
             and learning   I-78

Appendix 4: Administration and response rates   I-88

Appendix 5: The Questionnaires   I-91

PART II:
  **A REVIEW OF THE RESEARCH LITERATURE ON MOTIVATION
  TOWARDS SCHOOL AND LEARNING**

CHAPTER 1:   INTRODUCTION   II-3

**CHAPTER 2:   WHAT IS MOTIVATION TOWARDS SCHOOL
               AND LEARNING?**   II-4

**CHAPTER 3:   THE MEASUREMENT OF MOTIVATION
               TOWARDS SCHOOL AND LEARNING**   II-6

**CHAPTER 4:   FACTORS ASSOCIATED WITH MOTIVATION
               TOWARDS SCHOOL AND LEARNING**   II-7

**CHAPTER 5:   STRATEGIES TO IMPROVE STUDENTS'
               MOTIVATION, BEHAVIOUR, ACHIEVEMENTS
               & FUTURE PROSPECTS**   II-19

CHAPTER 6:   SUMMARY AND CONCLUSIONS   II-27

REFERENCES   II-31

ACKNOWLEDGEMENTS

This study could not have been completed without the help of a large number of people and we would like to express our thanks to:

* The students, teachers and headteachers in the schools which took part in the study;

* Members of the National Commission on Education's Working Group on Schools and Citizenship, whose names are given in Appendix 1, for their advice and suggestions;

* Professor Peter Mortimore of the Institute of Education, London University and Professor Andrew McPherson, Co-director of the Centre for Educational Sociology, University of Edinburgh, who read and commented on the draft report;

* Barry Wakefield, Deputy Director of the National Commission on Education, and Sue Taylor, Research Officer to the Commission, for their unfailing help and support at all stages of the research;

* Ray Sumner, Dougal Hutchison, Neil Rubra and David Upton, who read and commented on the draft report;

* Barbara Bloomfield, Anne Milne and their colleagues in NFER's Field Research Services Department, who organised the administration of the study;

* Mary Hargreaves who prepared the layout, Tim Wright, who designed the cover and Enver Carim, who coordinated the production of the report;

* Pauline Pearce, Jane Westing and Maura Williams-Stock, who typed the manuscript.

FOREWORD

In its ambitious investigation of the capacity of our education service to meet the demands it will face over the next 25 years, the National Commission on Education has endeavoured to cover a huge spectrum of concerns and all phases of education from pre-school to higher education and beyond. Members of the Commission have considered reports and have gathered evidence from a variety of sources: from policy makers, practitioners and researchers not only in education but also in business and industry and many other fields. This report differs in one crucial respect from much of the material submitted to the Commission: it expresses the views of young people themselves about their experiences in schools today.

There is justifiable anxiety – both professional and public – about young people who find school an alienating experience. One of the Commission's aspirations is to find ways of ensuring that in future, learning becomes a rewarding experience for everyone. A desire to find out what proportion of young people lack motivation towards school, and what factors might cause them to lose interest in learning, prompted us to commission this study by the National Foundation for Educational Research. The results offer some fascinating insights, sometimes disturbing, sometimes encouraging. Assumptions about widespread disaffection, and the influence of socio-economic factors on motivation towards education, will be challenged by the report: there are indications here of high expectations of learning and strong support for the value of schools. There are also, however, inescapable signs of disenchantment with certain aspects of school life and school work.

Interpreting the results of the study will not be straightforward – it is understandably difficult to draw unequivocal messages from attitude surveys of this kind. The particular significance of this report is that it gives us a picture of secondary school life, good points and bad, from the students' perspective, and a sense of the worth they place on their education.

Alongside the wealth of other evidence considered by the Commission, it will help to suggest directions in which teaching and management practices in schools can be developed in future, in order to motivate and sustain students' interest in learning throughout their school careers, and indeed in later life.

Margaret Maden
Member of the National Commission on Education and
Chair of the Commission's Working Group on Schools, Society and Citizenship.

PART I

AN INVESTIGATION OF THE MOTIVATION TOWARDS SCHOOL AND LEARNING OF SECONDARY SCHOOL STUDENTS

CHAPTER 1

INTRODUCTION

1.1 The background to the study

The study described in this report was undertaken by the National Foundation for Educational Research to provide evidence to assist the Working Group on Schools, Society and Citizenship of the National Commission on Education in the formulation of its recommendations.

One of the major concerns of the Commission's Working Group on Schools, Society and Citizenship is the lack of interest in education, and even hostility towards school, evinced by a substantial minority of secondary school students. The Working Group has hypothesised that students' attitudes towards school and learning, which are mainly positive in Year 7, will become less positive by the time they reach Year 9. The working group acknowledges that the onset of puberty and the related uncertainty about being a child or a young person may well be a contributory factor in any decline in motivation amongst many 13-year-olds, but argues that schooling also plays a part since Year 9 falls between two marked phases when pupils receive greater attention: the induction process for younger students who have just moved up from primary schools; and the more specialised examination-oriented options course structure of Years 10 and 11. The Working Group points out that many students may find it very difficult to re-engage fully with the purposes of school and education if their interest and motivation are allowed to slip in Year 9 and that 'without positive encouragement from parents and teachers, the 13-year-old can lose any clear sense of direction and purpose'.

The main aims of the research described in this report were to investigate the experiences and attitudes of 11-and 13-year-old students in their schools in order to:

- test the hypothesis that students' levels of motivation towards schooling are lower in Year 9 than in Year 7;

- identify the factors associated with motivation towards school and learning and hypothesise causes for hostility towards school;

- highlight those results which are most likely to assist the Commission's Working Party on Schools, Society and Citizenship in the formulation of its recommendations.

The research consisted of two complementary components which, because of the short time scale of the study, were carried out concurrently. The main component, which is described in Part I of this report, consisted of questionnaire surveys of Year 7 and Year 9 students in maintained, grant-maintained and independent schools in England and Wales, supplemented by a brief background questionnaire for schools. The second component of the research consisted of a review of previous research into motivation towards school and learning. This is described in Part II of this report.

1.2   The structure of Part I of the report

The following chapter describes the design of the study and the development and content of the questionnaires and gives details of the sampling and administration procedures. The next three chapters are concerned with the results of the analyses: Chapter 3 describes the background information provided by the students and schools which took part in the study; Chapter 4 compares the responses of the Year 7 and Year 9 students to a range of questions concerned with their experiences and behaviour in school and their attitudes towards school and schooling; and Chapter 5 reports on the associations found between students' attitudes towards school and a range of home, student, school and teaching measures. The final chapter provides an overview of the study and its background and highlights those results which are most likely to assist the Commission's Working Party on Schools, Society and Citizenship in the formulation of its recommendations.

CHAPTER 2
THE DESIGN AND ADMINISTRATION OF THE STUDY

The main purpose of this short chapter is to describe how the research was carried out and to give a brief description of the main issues covered in the questionnaires for students and schools.

2.1   The design of the research

The study consisted of questionnaire surveys of students in Years 7 and 9, complemented by a questionnaire seeking a small amount of background information from schools.

The questionnaire for students, which was substantially the same for both age groups, was developed from several different sources (Gray, McPherson and Raffe, 1983; MacBeath and Weir, 1991; Brighouse, 1992; and a range of previous surveys undertaken by NFER). We are grateful to those concerned for allowing us to use their materials.   Questions were adopted or adapted, as appropriate, and the draft questionnaires were piloted on a sample of 72 students in Years 7 and 9 in three schools. The questionnaire was amended in the light of the pilot study.

2.2   The content of the questionnaires

The main topics covered in the questionnaires for students were:

- **background variables** including: gender; surrogate measures intended to provide an approximate indication of the cultural level of the home; perceived ability and behaviour in school; and post-16 educational intentions;

- **attitudes towards school and learning** including: views about the value of school and school work; liking for school; interest and boredom with school work; and opinions on the purposes of schooling;

- **perceptions of teachers and lessons** including: liking for teachers; teachers' support of students' learning; teachers' maintenance of discipline; individual discussions with teachers about school work and career plans; and liking for different types of lessons;

- **students' self-reported behaviour in and out of school** including: behaviour in school; punishments; truancy; participation in lunch hour or after school activities; length of time spent doing homework, reading for pleasure; and watching television or videos.

- **perceptions of parental interest and home support** including: parents' opinions about the value of education; parental interest in students' progress at school; parental encouragement of good behaviour in school; parental aspirations; discussion of career plans with their parents, family and friends.

The students' questionnaire consisted of two main types of question. In the first part of the questionnaire students were asked to indicate their level of agreement with each of a number of statements by circling a number on a five-point scale either:

strongly agree/ agree/ not sure/ disagree/ strongly disagree; **or**

all lessons/ most lessons/ some lessons/ hardly any lessons/ no lessons; **or**

always/ nearly always/ sometimes/ hardly ever/ never/ **or**

all teachers/ most teachers/ some teachers/ hardly any teachers/ no teachers

as appropriate to the content of the statement.

Most of the remainder of the questionnaire consisted of 'closed' questions which required students to select one or more pre-coded responses by circling a number or ticking a box.

The main topics covered in the questionnaires for schools were:

- background information, including type of catchment area, percentages of students receiving free school meals and from ethnic minorities, and the approximate proportion of the intake with reading ages more than two years behind chronological ages;

- examination results in Years 11 and 13 and proportions of Year 13 leavers going on to higher education;

- consultation, reviewing and recording procedures used to support the progress of Key Stage 3 students.

Most of the questions in the school questionnaire asked schools either to enter a number or a percentage in a box or to select one or more pre-coded responses by circling a number or a tick.

Copies of the questionnaires are shown in Appendix 5.

2.3   Sampling, administration and response rates

In order to minimise the workload on individual schools, separate samples of schools were drawn for the surveys of Year 7 students (Sample A in Tables 3.1-3.6) and Year 9 students (Sample B). The samples of schools for each age group were drawn from schools containing students of that age group (with a probability proportional to the size of the age group in the school) from the Register of Schools, an annually updated database of all schools in England and Wales maintained by the NFER. The samples of schools were stratified by size (in terms of the numbers of pupils in the relevant age group), type of school (comprehensive to 16, comprehensive to 18, other secondary and independent), region (North, Midlands, South) and type of LEA (metropolitan, non-metropolitan).

It was intended to achieve two samples, each containing about 1000 students in approximately 50 schools. Previous experience suggested that the response rate from secondary schools in the summer term would be about 70 per cent. The initial samples drawn from the Register of Schools, therefore, each consisted of 75 schools.

The administration of the study, which took place in summer 1992, was undertaken by NFER's Field Research Services Department. All schools selected for the samples were invited to take part in the study and asked to provide NFER with a list of tutor groups in either Year 7 or Year 9, as appropriate. One tutor group was randomly selected by NFER from each participating school and questionnaires for that tutor group were dispatched to the school. The headteacher of each school was also asked to arrange for the completion of a brief school background questionnaire. The short timescale of the study only allowed time to send one reminder at each stage.

Tables A4.1 and A4.2 in Appendix 4 provide full details of the numbers of schools invited to take part in the study and of the achieved samples and response rates. The achieved samples, which were very close in size to our intended samples, consisted of 1160 Year 7 students in 47 schools and 980 Year 9 students in 43 schools. This represented response rates of 66 per cent and 61 per cent, respectively, from the schools initially approached for the Year 7 and Year 9 samples, and 92 per cent and 93 per cent, respectively, from the schools which had agreed to take part. Overall, 83 schools (44 in the Year 7 sample and 39 in the Year 9 sample) completed the background questionnaire for schools. The lower response rate from the Year 9 sample was not unexpected since the survey took place immediately after the Pilot National Curriculum Assessment at Key Stage 3.

The data were analysed by the NFER's Statistics Department, using appropriate statistical packages. In order to reduce any bias due to non-response, the samples were weighted to reflect the national distribution of students in terms of school-type (Comprehensive; Independent; Others), area (Metropolitan; Non-metropolitan) and region (North; Midlands; South).

CHAPTER 3
THE STUDENTS AND THE SCHOOLS

3.1 Introduction

This chapter describes and compares the samples of students and schools which participated in the study.

In the previous chapter, we explained that we had selected separate samples of schools for the Year 7 survey (Sample A) and Year 9 survey (Sample B) in order to minimise the workload on schools and, thus, ensure a good response to the study. One of the disadvantages of this approach is that the two achieved samples may differ in terms of factors, such as type of catchment area of the school and home background of the students, which have been shown by the previous research, described in Part II of this report, to affect students' achievement and motivation towards school and education.

In order to ensure that any conclusions drawn from the results of this study with regard to differences in the attitudes and behaviour of Year 7 and Year 9 students cannot be explained by differences between the two samples in catchment area or intake, it is necessary to make certain that there are no substantial differences between the two samples of schools (and of students) in terms of catchment area and other background factors.

One of the purposes of this chapter, therefore, is to examine the similarities and differences between the two achieved samples of schools, in terms of type of intake, catchment area and results in public examinations and between the two samples of students in terms of home background factors.

The samples of schools and students which participated in the study were, therefore, compared under the following main headings:

- catchment area and intake information provided by the schools;

- information on examination results provided by the schools;

- information on consultation, reviewing and reporting procedures provided by the schools;

- background information provided by the students.

The school background questionnaire was returned by 83 of the 90 schools taking part in the study.

The chi-squared test or t-tests, as appropriate, have been used to determine the statistical significance of any differences between the two samples. The five per cent level of statistical significance has been accepted as evidence of difference between the two year groups.

3.2 Catchment area and intake information provided by the schools

The schools taking part in the study were asked to provide information on their catchment area, the percentages of students receiving free school meals and from ethnic minorities, and the approximate proportion of the intake with reading ages more than two years behind chronological ages. Their responses are shown in Tables 3.1 and 3.2.

Table 3.1   Type of catchment area: comparisons between the schools in Sample A and Sample B

	Sample A		Sample B	
Total..	44	100%	39	100%
Mainly country town and/or rural.....	18	41%	15	40%
Mainly suburban...............................	14	31%	14	38%
Mainly urban/inner city.....................	13	28%	9	22%
Missing response..............................	0	0%	1	0%

The Year 7 sample of students was selected from Sample A schools and the Year 9 sample of students from Sample B schools.
No. of schools not completing the questionnaire: 7 (3 in Sample A, 4 in Sample B.)

Table 3.1 shows that overall about 40 per cent of the schools described their catchment area as 'mainly country town and/or rural', about a third selected 'mainly suburban' and just over a quarter opted for 'mainly urban/inner city'. The proportion of urban/inner city schools was slightly higher in Sample A (28 per cent, compared with 22 per cent) and the proportion of suburban schools slightly higher in Sample B (38 per cent, compared with 31 per cent). However, these differences were not statistically significant.

Similarly, there were very few differences between the two samples on the other catchment area variables (Table 3.2). The mean percentages of students from ethnic minorities in the Samples A and B were 7 per cent and 8 per cent, respectively, and the mean percentages of students receiving free school meals were 13 per cent in Sample A and 11 per cent in Sample B. The mean percentages of Year 7 students with reading ages more than two years behind their chronological ages at the beginning of Year 7 were 15 per cent in Sample A and 17 per cent in Sample B. None of these differences were statistically significant.

Table 3.2   Other catchment area and intake variables: comparisons between the schools in Sample A and Sample B

	Sample	Mean	s.d	N
Percentage of students from ethnic minorities	A	7.3	12.9	41
	B	7.5	13.1	38
Percentage of students receiving free school meals	A	13.3	11.8	41
	B	11.1	9.8	38
Percentage of Year 7 students with reading age more than 2 years behind chronological age	A	14.8	9.3	38
	B	17.0	11.5	30

None of these differences was statistically significant.
The Year 7 sample of students was selected from Sample A schools and the Year 9 sample of students from Sample B.
Only 30 of the 39 Sample B schools completing the questionnaire included Year 7 students.

3.3 Information on examination results provided by the schools

The schools taking part in the study were asked to provide information on examination results in Years 11 and 13 and proportions of Year 13 leavers going on to higher education. Their responses are shown in Table 3.3.

The differences between the two samples of schools in terms of Year 11 results were quite small. The mean percentages of Year 11 students gaining five or more higher grade (A-C) GCSEs in 1990/91 in samples A and B were 39 per cent and 35 per cent, respectively. The mean percentages of students in last year's Year 11 who, as far as their schools were aware, continued their full-time education were 63 per cent and 54 per cent, respectively (Table 3.3). These differences, which slightly favoured Sample A, were not statistically significant. It should be noted that only 32 of the 44 Year 7 sample schools returning the questionnaire contained Year 11 students. These comparisons could not, therefore, be made on the whole sample.

Table 3.3   Examination results and other output measures in Years 11 and 13: comparisons between Sample A and Sample B

	Sample	Mean	s.d	N
Percentage of students gaining 5 or more grades A-C GCSEs	A	38.5	24.2	31
	B	34.8	23.3	37
Percentage of students continuing their full-time education after Year 11	A	62.7	22.0	30
	B	54.0	26.0	35
Percentage of students obtaining two or more A-level passes grades A-E	A	77.4	17.2	20
	B	79.6	20.3	20
Percentage of students going on to higher education	A	70.8	18.5	20
	B	68.2	22.0	20

None of these differences was statistically significant.
The Year 7 sample of students was selected from Sample A schools and the Year 9 sample of students from Sample B schools.
Only 32 of Sample A and 37 of Sample B schools completing the questionnaire included Year 11 students.
Only 20 of Sample A and 21 of Sample B schools completing the questionnaire included Year 13 students.

The percentages shown in Table 3.3 are very close to the national averages, suggesting that our samples of schools are reasonably representative of all schools in England: comparable figures for all schools in England in 1990/91(DFE Statistical Bulletin 15/92) were: 36.8 per cent of 16-year-olds achieved 5 or more GCSE grades A-C; 63.6 per cent of all 16-year-olds either stayed on at school or entered full-time further or higher education.

After we had completed the research, the Department for Education published the 1992 A-level and GCSE results for maintained (and some independent) schools in England (*The Guardian*, November 19 1992). The published results included the percentage of students in the age group attaining five or more GCSE grade A-C passes in each school. These data allowed us to compare the average results of the non-responding schools in each sample with those of the schools which took part in the study (shown in Table 3.3). However, these comparisons should be regarded with caution, since information was unavailable for eight of the 22 non-responding schools in Sample A and six of the 29 non-responding schools in Sample B (schools in Wales, independent schools and, in Sample A only, middle schools).

For both samples, the mean percentage of students achieving five or more GCSE grade A-C passes in the non-responding schools was slightly higher than in the corresponding achieved sample (42.0 per cent compared with 38.5 per cent for Sample A and 43.1 per cent compared with 34.8 per cent for Sample B). However, these differences were not statistically significant. There was, therefore, no evidence that high- or low-achieving schools were over-represented in our achieved samples.

The differences between the two samples in terms of the Year 13 results, which favour Sample B, were also quite small (Table 3.3). The mean percentages of Year 13 students obtaining two or more A-level grades A-E or equivalent in Summer 1991 were 77 per cent in Sample A, and 80 per cent in Sample B, and the mean percentages of students going on to some form of higher education were 71 per cent in Sample A and 68 per cent in Sample B. These differences were not statistically significant. It should be noted that only 20 of the 44 Sample A schools and 21 of the 39 Sample B schools which returned the questionnaire contained Year 13 students. These comparisons could not, therefore, be made on the whole sample.

3.4 Information on consultation, reviewing and reporting procedures provided by the schools

The schools were asked to provide information on the consultation, reviewing and recording procedures used to support the progress of Key Stage 3 students. The responses of Sample A in respect of Year 7 students and those of Sample B in respect of Year 9 students are shown in Table 3.4.

Table 3.4 Monitoring and recording students' progress: the responses of Sample A and Sample B schools

	Sample A		Sample B	
	Monitoring Year 7 students' progress		Monitoring Year 9 students' progress	
Total..	44	(100%)	39	(100%)
Individual Action Plan (IAP)......	7	(16%)	5	(12%)
Records of Achievement (RoA) or RoA **and** profiling.......	23	(52%)	24	(61%)
Profiling without RoA................	10	(23%)	6	(15%)
Other..	13	(30%)	11	(28%)
None..	4	(9%)	3	(8%)

The Year 7 sample of students was selected from Sample A schools and the Year 9 sample of students from Sample B schools.
Percentages may sum to more than 100, since schools were able to select more than one response.

Overall, more than half of the schools in both samples used Records of Achievement (some of these also indicated that they used profiling) schemes; about a fifth indicated that they used profiling without Records of Achievement; slightly fewer said they used Individual Action Plans; and about 30 per cent indicated that they used some other method. As noted above many schools said that they used more than one approach.

Table 3.5 shows the proportions of schools providing their Year 7 or Year 9 students (as appropriate) with individual one-to-one review/target setting sessions. About half of Sample A schools provided individual sessions for all Year 7 students and about one fifth for some students; about one fifth did not provide such sessions. Nearly 60 per cent of Sample B schools provided such sessions for all Year 9 students; just over a quarter for some; about 10 per cent did not provided such sessions for Year 9 students.

Table 3.5 One-to-one review or target setting sessions (either with form group tutor or another teacher): the response of Sample A and Sample B schools.

	Sample A		Sample B	
	Reviewing Year 7 students' progress		Reviewing Year 9 students' progress	
Total:......................................	44	(100%)	39	(100%)
All students..............................	24	(55%)	23	(59%)
Some students...........................	9	(20%)	11	(28%)
No students...............................	8	(18%)	4	(10%)
Missing.....................................	3	(7%)	1	(3%)

The Year 7 sample of students were selected from Sample A schools and the Year 9 sample of students from Sample B schools.

Table 3.6 shows the amount of time schools allocated to one-to-one review. The majority of schools (about half of both samples) allocated less than 30 minutes per annum per student for such sessions; about a quarter allocated 30-60 minutes; and less than 10 per cent gave more than an hour.

Table 3.6 Minimum amount of time per student for one-to-one review in 1991/92: the responses of Sample A and Sample B schools

	Sample A		Sample B	
	Time allocated to Year 7 students		Time allocated to Year 9 students	
Total..	44	(100%)	39	(100%)
Over 60 minutes.........................	4	(9%)	2	(5%)
30 - 60 minutes.........................	9	(20%)	12	(31%)
Less than 30 minutes..................	20	(46%)	21	(54%)
Not applicable (no one-to-one review).............	6	(14%)	4	(10%)
Missing.....................................	5	(11%)	0	(0%)

The Year 7 sample of students were selected from Sample A schools and the Year 9 sample of students from Sample B schools.

3.5 Background information provided by the students

The students taking part in the study provided information on a number of background variables concerning themselves and their homes. These included personal details, such as gender and number of brothers and sisters, and a surrogate measure intended to give an approximate indication of the cultural level of the home.

3.5.1 Background information on the students and their homes

The students' responses to the questions seeking background information on them and their families are shown in the table below.

Table 3.7   Personal details: the responses of Year 7 and Year 9 students

	Year group			
	Year 7		Year 9	
Total..................................	1160	100.0%	980	100.0%
Sex				
Male..	596	51.4%	453	46.2%
Female..	543	46.8%	505	51.5%
Missing.......................................	21	1.8%	22	2.3%
No. of brothers and sisters				
Five or more................................	45	3.8%	48	4.8%
Four...	35	3.0%	51	5.2%
Three..	137	11.8%	127	12.9%
Two..	318	27.4%	255	26.0%
One..	545	47.0%	428	43.7%
None or missing...........................	81	7.0%	72	7.3%

Although Sample A contained a slightly higher proportion of boys and Sample B a slightly higher proportion of girls, these differences were not statistically significant. Neither were there any statistically significant differences in terms of family size. The majority of the students had either one (47 per cent of the Year 7 students and 44 per cent of those in Year 9) or two (27 per cent and 26 per cent respectively) brothers or sisters.

Previous studies (for example Comber and Keeves, 1973; Keys, 1987) have shown that a simple scale based on the approximate number of books in the home provides a useful surrogate measure of the cultural background of the home. The students taking part in this study were, therefore, asked to make a rough estimate of the number of books in their homes. The purpose of including this question was twofold: firstly, it was intended to allow us to compare the Year 7 and Year 9 students in terms of the cultural level of the home; and, secondly, it was intended to provide an indication of how well the samples of students reflected the populations from which they were drawn (all students in their age groups in independent and maintained schools in England and Wales). The students' responses are shown in Table 3.8, together with those from a previous nationally representative study (Keys, 1987).

Table 3.8   **Number of books in the home: the responses of Year 7 and Year 9 students compared with those from a previous nationally representative study**

	Present study		Previous study*	
Number of books in the home	Year 7 %	Year 9 %	Year 6 %	Year 9 %
0 - 10..........................	4	6	5	4
11 - 25..........................	12	10	11	10
26 - 100	25	28	31	31
101 - 250..........................	23	22	23	27
251 - 500	18	15	16	15
More than 500.....................	18	20	14	13
	100	100	100	100
No. of students responding.	1142	959	3556	2972
No. missing.......................	18	21	194	140
Total in sample..................	1160	980	3750	3112

The students not answering this question have been excluded from the percentages in order to make exact comparisons with the previous study.

* *The Second IEA Science Study (Keys, 1987)*

There were no statistically significant differences in the responses of the Year 7 and Year 9 students to this question. Table 3.8 also shows that the distribution of responses in the present study was consistent to the distribution in the earlier study. Thus, there appears to be no obvious reason to suggest lack of representativeness in the samples in terms of the cultural level of the students' homes.

3.6 Summary

i.   There were no statistically significant differences between the Year 7 and Year 9 samples of schools in terms of type of catchment area or intake variables, such as percentages of students from ethnic minorities or receiving school meals and reading age in Year 7.

ii. There were no statistically significant differences between the Year 7 and Year 9 samples of schools in terms of GCSE results and retention rates in Year 11. The percentages of 16 year olds in our sample gaining five or more GCSEs grades A-C, and percentages staying on in education were very close to the averages for England given in DES Statistical Bulletin 15/92.

iii. There were no statistically significant differences between the two samples in terms of A-level results and proportions going on to higher education. However, these comparisons were based on small numbers of schools since substantial proportions of the schools taking part in the study did not contain Year 13 students.

iv. There were no statistically significant differences between the Year 7 and Year 9 samples of students in terms of gender, family size or cultural level of the home.

CHAPTER 4

A COMPARISON OF THE RESPONSES OF YEAR 7 AND YEAR 9 STUDENTS

4.1 Introduction

One of the hypotheses outlined by the working party was that students' attitudes towards school and learning, which are mainly positive when they start secondary school in Year 7, become less positive by the time they reach Year 9.

The main purpose of this chapter is to test this hypothesis by comparing the responses of Year 7 and Year 9 students to the self-completion questionnaire concerned with their feelings and perceptions about different aspects of school life and their own behaviour in school.

The ideal design for a study of this nature would have been a longitudinal one, in which the same pupils were followed up over the two-year period, but cost and timing ruled this out. As an alternative, we originally considered a cross-sectional design in which the Year 7 and Year 9 samples came from the same schools: this would have had the benefit that some of the differences arising from random sampling of schools would have been removed. In the event, as noted earlier, it was decided that this would be too great a load to place on the schools, and separate school samples were picked for the two year groups.

This had the effect of confounding the year-group variable with the sample of schools picked (ie differences between the samples for the two year groups could be due to differences in the samples of schools picked rather than to any genuine differences between the two year groups). For this reason, it was important to compare the characteristics of the schools selected in the two year-groups. These comparisons, which are described in Chapter 3, show that there were no statistically significant differences between the two samples.

The students' responses have been discussed under the following main headings:

- Attitudes towards school and learning

- Teachers, teaching and discipline

- Students' self-reported ability and behaviour

- Parental and home support

Comparisons between the two age groups have normally been made in terms of the combined percentages selecting the two positive options (strongly agree and agree). Where appropriate, differences between the percentages selecting the most positive option (strongly agree) have been highlighted.

The information is presented in Tables 4.1 to 4.20. Levels of statistical significance have not been given in these tables since readily available coefficients, such as chi-squared or t-tests, would have been inappropriate because of the design of the study. However, Table A3.4 in Appendix 3 (which uses multilevel modelling (Goldstein, 1987) in order to take account of the hierarchical organisation of the data, and of the fact that students within the same schools are on average more similar than students in different schools) shows that year group was a significant factor in explaining differences in students' attitudes towards school.

4.2   Attitudes towards school and learning

There is evidence from the previous research literature described in Part II of this report that disillusion with education, dislike of school and boredom with schoolwork are associated with early leaving and dropout, and that a belief in the importance of education, liking for school and interest in schoolwork are associated with staying on (Part II, Sections 2.2 and 4.3). The questionnaire, therefore, included a number of statements concerned with students' attitudes towards school and school work. These focused on students' like and dislike of school, their interest in and boredom with school work, their perceptions of the value of school, schoolwork and the reputation of their school, and their views on the purposes of schooling.

4.2.1   Like and dislike of school

The four statements shown in Table 4.1 focused on like and dislike of school.

The majority of students appeared to like school reasonably well. Differences between the responses of the two age groups were quite small (Table 4.1). Nevertheless, the Year 7 students were more likely to respond positively (strongly agree or agree) to the statement 'I am very happy when I am at school' (68 per cent compared with 60 per cent of Year 9 students) and less likely to respond negatively (11 per cent compared with 21 per cent). They were also more likely to express strong agreement with 'On the whole, I like being at school'. The students' responses to this question suggest that, although the majority are reasonably favourably disposed towards school, about 12 per cent of students in Year 7 and 13 per cent of those in Year 9 (the proportions strongly disagreeing or disagreeing with the statement: 'On the whole, I like being at school') may be hostile towards school.

Table 4.1   Like and dislike of school: the views of Year 7 and Year 9 students

	Year group			
	Year 7		Year 9	
Total..	1160	100.0%	980	100.0%
I am very happy when I am at school.				
Strongly agree.....................................	118	10.2%	45	4.5%
Agree..	669	57.7%	546	55.7%
Not sure...	236	20.3%	178	18.2%
Disagree...	104	9.0%	171	17.4%
Strongly disagree................................	28	2.4%	30	3.1%
Missing..	4	.4%	10	1.0%
On the whole I like being at school.				
Strongly agree.....................................	238	20.5%	115	11.7%
Agree..	658	56.8%	624	63.7%
Not sure...	117	10.1%	106	10.8%
Disagree...	99	8.5%	94	9.6%
Strongly disagree................................	42	3.6%	36	3.7%
Missing..	6	.6%	6	.6%
Most of the time I don't want to go to school.				
Strongly agree.....................................	111	9.5%	81	8.3%
Agree..	236	20.3%	233	23.8%
Not sure...	136	11.7%	103	10.5%
Disagree...	475	41.0%	434	44.3%
Strongly disagree................................	188	16.2%	120	12.2%
Missing..	14	1.2%	9	.9%
Do you like school:				
more than you did last year..............	..	..	446	45.5%
about the same as you did last year...	..	..	350	35.8%
less than you did last year.................	..	..	175	17.8%
Missing..	..	..	9	0.9%

On the other hand, their responses to the statement 'Most of the time I don't want to go to school' might suggest that the proportion of hostile students is higher: about 30 per cent of both age groups agreed they did not want to go to school; 60 per cent disagreed; the remainder were not sure. There were no differences between the responses of the two groups to this statement.

Surprisingly, 46 per cent of the Year 9 students said that they liked school more this year than they did last year and 36 per cent said that they liked school the same as last year. Only 18 per cent said that they liked school less. The reason for this apparent contradiction with the results from our comparisons between the responses of Year 7 and Year 9 students is unclear.

4.2.2   Interest or boredom in lessons

The three statements shown in Table 4.2 were concerned with interest or boredom in lessons.

Table 4.2   Interest or boredom in lessons: the views of Year 7 and Year 9 students

	Year group			
	Year 7		Year 9	
Total...	1160	100.0%	980	100.0%
The work I do in lessons is interesting to me.				
All lessons.....................................	142	12.3%	42	4.3%
Most lessons...................................	576	49.7%	499	50.9%
Some lessons...................................	369	31.8%	387	39.5%
Hardly any lessons..........................	52	4.5%	45	4.6%
No lessons......................................	9	.8%	1	.1%
Missing..	11	.9%	6	.6%
I am bored in lessons.				
All lessons.....................................	31	2.7%	14	1.4%
Most lessons...................................	61	5.2%	73	7.5%
Some lessons...................................	464	40.0%	536	54.7%
Hardly any lessons..........................	453	39.0%	310	31.6%
No lessons......................................	133	11.5%	34	3.5%
Missing..	18	1.6%	12	1.2%
In a lesson, I often count the minutes till it ends.				
All lessons.....................................	80	6.9%	69	7.0%
Most lessons...................................	102	8.8%	126	12.9%
Some lessons...................................	398	34.3%	405	41.3%
Hardly any lessons..........................	332	28.7%	281	28.7%
No lessons......................................	240	20.7%	94	9.6%
Missing..	7	.6%	5	.5%

Overall, the students' responses to the three statements concerned with interest or boredom in lessons were less positive than their responses to the statements concerned with liking for school. In addition, the responses of the Year 7 students were more positive than those of the Year 9 students (Table 4.2). For example, 51 per cent of the Year 7 students, compared with only 35 per cent of those in Year 9, indicated that they were never or hardly ever bored in lessons (a difference of 16 percentage points) and about 62 per cent of the Year 7 students, compared with only 55 per cent of the Year 9 students, agreed that the work they did in all or most lessons was interesting.

The responses of both groups of students suggested that they perceived some lessons as boring, although once again the responses of the Year 7 students were more positive. For example, about 16 per cent of the Year 7 students and 20 per cent of the Year 9 students said that they often counted the minutes to the end of all or most lessons and a further 34 per cent and 41 per cent, respectively, indicated that they did so in some lessons.

4.2.3   The value of school and school work

Three statements were concerned with the value of school and school work. The students' responses are shown in Table 4.3.

The majority of the students in both age groups responded very positively to these statements. For example over 90 per cent agreed or strongly agreed that school work was worth doing and only about three per cent believed that the work they did was a waste of time in all or most lessons or that school itself was a waste of time (Table 4.3).

In terms of overall positive responses (the percentages opting for 'strongly agree' and 'agree' combined), there was very little difference between the responses of the two age groups to the statement 'School work is worth doing', although the Year 7 students were more likely to disagree with the statement that the work they did in lessons was a waste of time (84 per cent of the Year 7 students, compared with only 73 per cent of those in Year 9 strongly disagreed or disagreed with this statement). However, closer investigation revealed that the Year 7 students were much more likely than those in Year 9 to opt for the most positive responses (i.e. 'strongly agreeing' that school work was worth doing and indicating that the work they did in 'no lessons' was a waste of time). No differences were found in the responses of the two groups to the statement 'School is a waste of time for me'.

Table 4.3   **The value of school and school work: the views of Year 7 and Year 9 students**

	Year group			
	Year 7		Year 9	
Total...	1160	100.0%	980	100.0%
School work is worth doing.				
Strongly agree..................................	429	37.0%	286	29.2%
Agree..	628	54.1%	608	62.0%
Not sure..	42	3.6%	41	4.2%
Disagree...	31	2.7%	20	2.0%
Strongly disagree.............................	26	2.3%	20	2.0%
Missing...	5	.4%	6	.6%
The work I do in lessons is a waste of time.				
All lessons.......................................	12	1.1%	4	.4%
Most lessons....................................	27	2.3%	18	1.8%
Some lessons....................................	134	11.6%	233	23.8%
Hardly any lessons...........................	353	30.5%	422	43.0%
No lessons..	615	53.0%	290	29.6%
Missing...	18	1.6%	14	1.4%
School is a waste of time for me.				
Strongly agree..................................	18	1.6%	12	1.2%
Agree..	20	1.7%	21	2.1%
Not sure..	47	4.0%	32	3.3%
Disagree...	395	34.1%	367	37.5%
Strongly disagree.............................	676	58.3%	543	55.5%
Missing...	4	.4%	5	.5%

4.2.4   Students' perceptions of the purposes of school

Our review of the literature revealed that many students (and their parents) believed that an important purpose of school and education was to help students get a job or to set them on the path for their chosen career (Part II, Section 4.1.1). Five statements, therefore, focused on students' perceptions of the purposes of school. These are shown in Table 4.4.

All the students appeared to believe in the 'utilitarian' purposes of school (Table 4.4). The vast majority of the students (around 90 per cent in both age groups) strongly agreed or agreed that schools should help them to do well in exams, teach them things which would be useful when they got jobs and to be independent. Their most positive response (in terms of the percentage strongly agreeing) was concerned with doing well in examinations. There were no differences between the responses of the two age groups on these three issues.

However, in their responses to a statement focusing on what the school 'does', rather than 'should do', the Year 7 students were more positive than those in Year 9, even though the majority of both age groups (89 per cent and about 84 per cent, respectively) disagreed or strongly disagreed with the statement that 'School work doesn't help you get a job'.

The students were less certain about the importance of the school's role in helping them to learn how to use their leisure time: only about 40 per cent of the Year 7 students and 34 per cent of those in Year 9 strongly agreed or agreed with this statement. However, once again, the responses of the Year 7 students were more positive.

**Table 4.4   Students' perceptions of the purposes of school:
the views of Year 7 and Year 9 students**

	Year group			
	Year 7		Year 9	
Total..	1160	100.0%	980	100.0%
Schools should help us to do as well as possible in exams like GCSE.				
Strongly agree.............................	863	74.4%	754	77.0%
Agree...	258	22.2%	205	20.9%
Not sure.......................................	23	2.0%	8	.9%
Disagree.......................................	8	.7%	3	.3%
Strongly disagree.........................	4	.4%	5	.5%
Missing...	4	.3%	4	.4%
Schools should teach things that will be useful when we get jobs.				
Strongly agree.............................	713	61.4%	575	58.7%
Agree...	384	33.1%	361	36.9%
Not sure.......................................	42	3.6%	20	2.0%
Disagree.......................................	14	1.2%	13	1.4%
Strongly disagree.........................	3	.3%	5	.5%
Missing...	4	.3%	5	.5%
Schools should help us to be independent and stand on our own two feet.				
Strongly agree.............................	458	39.5%	376	38.4%
Agree...	567	48.8%	516	52.6%
Not sure.......................................	77	6.6%	39	4.0%
Disagree.......................................	44	3.8%	34	3.5%
Strongly disagree.........................	4	.4%	5	.5%
Missing...	10	.9%	10	1.0%
Schools should help us to learn how to use our spare time.				
Strongly agree.............................	153	13.2%	76	7.8%
Agree...	313	27.0%	259	26.4%
Not sure.......................................	174	15.0%	114	11.6%
Disagree.......................................	326	28.1%	321	32.7%
Strongly disagree.........................	189	16.3%	205	20.9%
Missing...	5	.4%	5	.5%
School work doesn't help you get a job.				
Strongly agree.............................	19	1.6%	14	1.4%
Agree...	48	4.1%	51	5.2%
Not sure.......................................	54	4.6%	82	8.4%
Disagree.......................................	330	28.5%	351	35.8%
Strongly disagree.........................	696	60.0%	476	48.5%
Missing...	13	1.1%	6	.7%

4.2.5 Students' comments on the purposes of school

The Year 9 students were asked to respond to the following open-ended question:

Thinking about your future, what are the most important ways your school could help you?

The majority (86 per cent) of the students commented, some mentioning more than one issue. Most of their comments were concerned with preparation for the future. The main points made under this heading, together with the percentages of the whole sample flagging each issue, are given below:

- **The acquisition of life skills**: encourage personal discipline and self-motivation; improve attitudes; help students reach their full potential; 'prepare you for the outside world'; develop future life skills, social skills or independence (24 per cent).

- **The provision of support and encouragement**: provide 'credit when we do something good'; one-to-one talks; help with general decisions; progress reports; options advice (21 per cent).

- **The provision of knowledge about careers**: careers advice; work experience; visits from professionals (19 per cent).

- **The provision of high quality education**: a good all-round education; students able to understand school work; 'teaching us new things'; 'teach me everything I need to know'; 'teach us the best they can'(18 per cent).

- **Help in gaining qualifications (for HE/FE or reason not specified)**: pass exams; do well in GCSEs; gain good grades for further and higher education (17 per cent).

- **Help in gaining (qualifications for) employment**: gain good qualifications for a job; get a job (17 per cent).

A small number of their comments focused on the school and lessons. These are shown below:

- **The provision of work-related education**: lessons focusing on vocational skills (6 per cent).

- **Improvements to lessons in various ways:** (6 per cent).

- **Wider subject choice**: better options (3 per cent).

- **Improved school management**: rules; resources (2 per cent).

- **Concentration on basic skills**: reading; writing (2 per cent)

4.2.6 Perceived reputation of their school

Two statements in the questionnaire were concerned with students' perceptions of the reputation of their school. These are shown in the table below.

Table 4.5   Perceived reputation of their school: the views of Year 7 and Year 9 students

	Year group			
	Year 7		Year 9	
Total...	1160	100.0%	980	100.0%
People think this is a good school.				
Strongly agree.................................	367	31.7%	189	19.3%
Agree...	560	48.2%	531	54.2%
Not sure...	142	12.2%	139	14.2%
Disagree...	58	5.0%	73	7.5%
Strongly disagree............................	21	1.8%	38	3.9%
Missing..	12	1.0%	9	.9%
My school is clean and tidy.				
Always..	210	18.1%	87	8.9%
Nearly always..................................	548	47.3%	413	42.1%
Sometimes..	280	24.1%	306	31.2%
Hardly ever......................................	69	6.0%	88	9.0%
Never..	43	3.7%	80	8.1%
Missing..	9	.8%	7	.7%

The Year 7 students were more likely than those in Year 9 to have favourable perceptions on the reputation of their school (Table 4.5). For example, 80 per cent of the Year 7 students, compared with 74 per cent of the Year 9 students, responded positively to the statement 'People think this is a good school'. They were also more likely to agree that their school was always or nearly always clean and tidy.

4.3 Teachers, teaching and the maintenance of discipline

The previous research, described in Part II of this report, has shown that good classroom management, effective support of students' learning and good discipline are associated with positive attitudes towards school and high achievement (Part II, Section 4.4). The questionnaire, therefore, contained a number of statements and questions concerned with teachers and teaching: liking for teachers; teacher support of students' learning; and the maintenance of discipline.

4.3.1 Liking for teachers

The students were asked to indicate whether they liked all, most, some, hardly any or no teachers (Table 4.6).

Table 4.6   Liking for teachers: the views of Year 7 and Year 9 students

	Year group			
	Year 7		Year 9	
Total..	1160	100.0%	980	100.0%
I like my teachers.				
All teachers.......................................	173	14.9%	43	4.4%
Most teachers....................................	525	45.3%	332	33.9%
Some teachers....................................	355	30.6%	458	46.8%
Hardly any teachers...........................	77	6.6%	109	11.2%
No teachers.......................................	22	1.9%	32	3.3%
Missing..	8	.7%	5	.5%

The responses of the Year 7 students were far more positive than those of the Year 9 students. About 60 per cent of Year 7 students, compared with just under 40 per cent of those in Year 9, said that they liked all or most of their teachers, a difference of 20 percentage points.

4.3.2 Ensuring the quality of students' work

The four statements shown in Table 4.7 relate to the strategies teachers used to ensure the quality of their students' work.

The students' responses to this set of statements reveal a pattern of more positive perceptions of their teachers' efforts to ensure the quality of students' work amongst Year 7 students (Table 4.7). In general, the majority in both groups of students agreed that their teachers always or usually marked their work (97 per cent and 92 per cent, respectively), that all or most of their teachers made sure they did any homework that is set (91 per cent and 84 per cent, respectively), and that their teachers tried hard to make them work as well as they were able (78 per cent and 71 per cent, respectively)

Table 4.7   Ensuring the quality of students' work: the views of Year 7 and Year 9 students

	Year group			
	Year 7		Year 9	
Total..	1160	100.0%	980	100.0%
Most of my teachers:				
always mark my work......................	444	38.3%	263	26.9%
usually mark my work.....................	676	58.3%	634	64.7%
hardly ever mark my work...............	35	3.0%	75	7.6%
Missing...	5	.4%	8	.8%
My teachers make sure we do any homework that is set .				
All teachers....................................	574	49.5%	261	26.6%
Most teachers.................................	484	41.7%	564	57.5%
Some teachers.................................	80	6.9%	129	13.1%
Hardly any teachers.........................	11	1.0%	18	1.9%
No teachers.....................................	6	.5%	2	.2%
Missing...	5	.4%	7	.7%
Most of my teachers:				
try hard to make me work as well as I am able..................................	905	78.0%	697	71.2%
are fairly easily satisfied..................	224	19.3%	249	25.4%
Don't seem to care whether I work or not...	24	2.1%	26	2.6%
Missing...	7	.6%	8	.8%
My teachers praise me when I do my school work well.				
All teachers....................................	213	18.4%	132	13.4%
Most teachers.................................	425	36.6%	353	36.1%
Some teachers.................................	330	28.4%	345	35.3%
Hardly any teachers.........................	131	11.3%	109	11.2%
No teachers.....................................	52	4.5%	35	3.5%
Missing...	9	.8%	5	.5%

Nevertheless, it should be noted that more than a quarter of the Year 9 students and nearly one fifth of those in Year 7 said that their teachers 'were fairly easily satisfied' and that about two per cent of both groups indicated that their teachers did not seem to care whether they worked or not. In addition, about eight per cent of the Year 9 students and three per cent of those in Year 7 said that their teachers hardly ever marked their work.

Another striking finding is that only 55 per cent of the Year 7 students and 50 per cent of those in Year 9 indicated that all or most of their teachers praised them when they did their work well.

4.3.3   Maintaining discipline

The six statements or questions shown in Table 4.8 focused on maintaining discipline within and outside the classroom.

Although the responses of the majority of students in both age groups were favourable to all the statements shown in Table 4.8, those of the Year 7 students tended to be more positive than those of the Year 9 students.

Year 7 students were more likely to perceive that their teachers were making efforts to maintain discipline. For example, 90 per cent of the Year 7 students, compared with 82 per cent of those in Year 9, indicated that all or most of their teachers made it clear how they should behave in school, and 87 per cent, compared with 80 per cent, agreed that all or most of their teachers took action when they saw anyone breaking the school rules.

The Year 7 students also appeared to rate the standard of discipline in their schools more highly . They were much more likely than those in Year 9 to agree that all or most of their teachers could keep order in class (76 per cent of the Year 7 students compared with 56 per cent of Year 9 students - a difference of 20 percentage points) and that their school had sensible rules (80 per cent and 61 per cent, respectively, a difference of 19 percentage points). Conversely, the Year 9 students were more likely to believe that the discipline in their school was too strict (19 per cent of Year 9 students, compared with only 12 per cent of those in Year 7) and that their school had too many rules (40 per cent and 21 per cent, respectively).

Table 4.8   Maintaining discipline: the views of Year 7 and Year 9 students

	Year group			
	Year 7		Year 9	
Total...................................	1160	100.0%	980	100.0%
The teachers take action when they see anyone breaking school rules.				
All teachers...................................	631	54.4%	352	35.9%
Most teachers.................................	381	32.8%	428	43.7%
Some teachers.................................	125	10.8%	170	17.3%
Hardly any teachers.........................	11	1.0%	21	2.1%
No teachers....................................	3	.2%	5	.5%
Missing...	9	.8%	5	.5%
My teachers make it clear how we should behave in school.				
All teachers...................................	687	59.2%	359	36.6%
Most teachers.................................	360	31.0%	447	45.7%
Some teachers.................................	97	8.3%	150	15.3%
Hardly any teachers.........................	12	1.0%	12	1.3%
No teachers....................................	1	.1%	2	.2%
Missing...	4	.3%	10	1.0%
My teachers can keep order in class.				
All teachers...................................	313	27.0%	62	6.3%
Most teachers.................................	564	48.7%	489	49.9%
Some teachers.................................	229	19.7%	348	35.5%
Hardly any teachers.........................	40	3.5%	59	6.0%
No teachers....................................	8	.7%	19	1.9%
Missing...	6	.5%	4	.4%
My school has sensible rules.				
Strongly agree.................................	209	18.0%	53	5.4%
Agree..	713	61.5%	546	55.7%
Not sure..	110	9.4%	103	10.5%
Disagree..	95	8.1%	222	22.6%
Strongly disagree............................	24	2.0%	50	5.1%
Missing...	10	.9%	7	.7%
Do you think the discipline in your school is:				
too strict?.....................................	140	12.1%	190	19.4%
about right?...................................	963	83.0%	717	73.2%
not strict enough?...........................	50	4.3%	59	6.0%
Missing...	7	.6%	14	1.4%
Does your school have:				
too many rules?..............................	237	20.5%	394	40.2%
about the right number of rules?.......	874	75.3%	549	56.1%
not enough rules?............................	42	3.6%	25	2.5%
Missing...	7	.6%	13	1.3%

4.3.4 Talking individually to teachers

The importance of clear and unanimous feedback in enhancing students' attitudes and achievement has been highlighted in previous research (Part II, Section 4.4). Four questions, therefore, focused on talking to teachers about work and career plans. These are shown in the table below.

Table 4.9 Talking individually to teachers: the responses of Year 7 and Year 9 students

	Year group			
	Year 7		Year 9	
Total..	1160	100.0%	980	100.0%
Have you talked to your class teacher about your work?				
Often..	77	6.6%	58	5.9%
Sometimes.......................................	460	39.7%	399	40.7%
Never...	504	43.5%	444	45.4%
Missing..	119	10.2%	79	8.0%
Have you talked to other teachers about your work?				
Often..	53	4.6%	70	7.2%
Sometimes.......................................	396	34.2%	443	45.2%
Never...	488	42.1%	406	41.4%
Missing..	222	19.1%	61	6.3%
Do you talk to your form tutor about your career plans?				
Often..	18	1.5%	44	4.5%
Sometimes.......................................	89	7.7%	283	28.8%
Never or hardly...............................	704	60.7%	515	52.5%
Missing..	350	30.1%	138	14.1%
Do you talk to any other teachers about your career plans?				
Often..	14	1.2%	41	4.1%
Sometimes.......................................	83	7.2%	262	26.7%
Never or hardly...............................	708	61.0%	535	54.5%
Missing..	354	30.6%	143	14.6%

The most striking finding is the high proportion of students in both year groups who say that they never or hardly ever talked individually to their teachers about their school work (about 40 per cent of both groups) or their career plans (60 per cent of Year 7 students and over 50 per cent of those in Year 9).

There were no differences in the proportions of students in Year 7 and Year 9 indicating that they had talked individually with their class/form teacher about their school work since the beginning of the school year: often (seven per cent and six per cent, respectively); sometimes (40 per cent and 41 respectively); never or hardly ever (44 per cent and 45 per cent, respectively). The Year 9 students were slightly more likely to have talked to other teachers about their work.

Not unexpectedly, in view of their age, the Year 9 students were more likely than those in Year 7 to have talked to teachers about their career plans. However, as stated above, about half of Year 9 students said that they never or hardly ever talked to their teachers about their career plans. This compares with only 7 per cent and 12 per cent, respectively, who said that they hardly ever discuss career plans with their parents and friends (Tables 4.15 and 4.16).

4.3.5   Types of lessons liked

Curriculum innovations, such as the Technical and Vocational Education Initiative (TVEI) and the Lower Attaining Pupils Programme (LAPP) have emphasised non-traditional teaching approaches and practical activities on the grounds that these are more likely to interest students and increase their motivation towards education. The questionnaire contained four statements concerned with teaching approaches. These are shown in Table 4.10.

Both age groups expressed the greatest preference for lessons where they could work with their friends (over 90 per cent strongly agreed or agreed that they liked this type of lesson). The second most highly rated type of lesson, especially liked by the Year 7 students, was one in which they could make something (90 per cent of the Year 7 students and 79 per cent of those in Year 9 strongly agreed or agreed that they liked this type of lesson) and their third choice was lessons in which they had discussions (three-quarters of both age groups strongly agreed or agreed that they liked this type of lesson). Interestingly, only about half of the students strongly agreed or agreed that they liked lessons where they could work on their own. Yet, in most secondary schools, this is the most frequent type of lesson provided.

Table 4.10   Types of lessons liked: the views of Year 7 and Year 9 students

	Year group			
	Year 7		Year 9	
Total....................................	1160	100.0%	980	100.0%
I like lessons where I can work with my friends .				
Strongly agree...............................	619	53.4%	426	43.5%
Agree..	455	39.2%	487	49.6%
Not sure.......................................	32	2.8%	27	2.7%
Disagree.......................................	32	2.7%	25	2.6%
Strongly disagree...........................	12	1.0%	7	.7%
Missing...	10	.8%	9	.9%
I like lessons where I can work on my own.				
Strongly agree...............................	173	14.9%	81	8.3%
Agree..	447	38.5%	417	42.6%
Not sure.......................................	132	11.4%	120	12.3%
Disagree.......................................	276	23.8%	277	28.3%
Strongly disagree...........................	125	10.8%	78	8.0%
Missing...	7	.6%	6	.6%
I like lessons where I can make something.				
Strongly agree...............................	544	46.9%	285	29.1%
Agree..	497	42.8%	493	50.3%
Not sure.......................................	46	4.0%	70	7.2%
Disagree.......................................	42	3.7%	90	9.2%
Strongly disagree...........................	17	1.5%	35	3.6%
Missing...	13	1.1%	7	.7%
I like lessons where we have discussions.				
Strongly agree...............................	351	30.2%	271	27.6%
Agree..	522	45.0%	470	48.0%
Not sure.......................................	115	9.9%	78	7.9%
Disagree.......................................	118	10.2%	124	12.7%
Strongly disagree...........................	47	4.1%	32	3.3%
Missing...	8	.7%	5	.5%

4.4 Students' behaviour in school and out-of-school activities

Our review of the literature identified a body of research linking disaffection towards school with poor self-image, disruptive behaviour, lack of interest in school work, truancy, early leaving and dropout (Part II, Sections 2.2 and 4.3.1).

4.4.1 Students' perceptions of their ability and perseverance

The questionnaire for students included four statements or questions focusing on the students' perceptions of their own ability and perseverance with school work. These are shown in Table 4.11.

There were no differences between the Year 7 and Year 9 students in terms of their perceptions of their own ability, their perceptions of their teachers' ratings of their ability or their responses to the statement 'I get good marks for my work'.

The students' perceptions of their own ability were quite high. About 40 per cent of both groups rated themselves as 'average', a few more as 'above average' and around 10 per cent indicated that they were 'very good'. Only about four per cent saw themselves as 'below average' or 'not at all good'. Their perceptions of their teachers' ratings of their ability were very slightly lower. Similarly, their reports of marks achieved were quite high: about 60 per cent of the students in both age groups reported getting good marks for their work in all or most lessons; a further 36 per cent in some lessons; only about four per cent indicated that they hardly ever or never obtained good marks (Table 4.11).

However, the Year 7 students were more likely than those in Year 9 to believe that they worked hard in school. About 86 per cent of the Year 7 students, compared with only 79 per cent of those in Year 9, indicated that they worked as hard as they could in all or most lessons (Table 4.11).

**Table 4.11   Perceptions of ability and perseverance:
the responses of Year 7 and Year 9 students**

	Year group			
	Year 7		Year 9	
Total.................................	1160	100.0%	980	100.0%
I work as hard as I can in school.				
All lessons.......................................	303	26.2%	132	13.5%
Most lessons....................................	690	59.4%	639	65.2%
Some lessons...................................	146	12.6%	187	19.1%
Hardly any lessons...........................	11	1.0%	13	1.3%
No lessons.......................................	3	.2%	3	.3%
Missing...	8	.7%	7	.7%
How good do you think you are at school work?				
Very good.......................................	134	11.5%	95	9.7%
Above average.................................	502	43.3%	411	41.9%
Average...	462	39.8%	403	41.1%
Below average.................................	38	3.3%	39	4.0%
Not at all good................................	13	1.1%	4	.4%
Missing...	11	1.0%	29	2.9%
How do you think your teachers would describe your school work?				
Very good.......................................	148	12.7%	117	12.0%
Above average.................................	411	35.5%	343	35.0%
Average...	501	43.2%	435	44.4%
Below average.................................	63	5.5%	44	4.5%
Not at all good................................	18	1.5%	6	.6%
Missing	19	1.6%	34	3.5%
I get good marks for my work.				
All lessons.......................................	92	8.0%	54	5.5%
Most lessons....................................	596	51.4%	525	53.6%
Some lessons...................................	408	35.2%	355	36.3%
Hardly any lessons...........................	43	3.7%	30	3.0%
No lessons.......................................	10	.8%	4	.4%
Missing...	10	.8%	11	1.1%

The students' responses to questions concerned with their post-16 intentions are shown in Table 4.12.

Table 4.12 Intention to remain in education beyond the statutory leaving age: the responses of Year 7 and Year 9 students

	Year group			
	Year 7		Year 9	
Total..	1160	100.0%	980	100.0%
After taking exams at the end of Year 11 do you expect to:				
go into the sixth form of this school.?	419	36.1%	327	33.3%
go to another school or college?......	303	26.1%	359	36.5%
get a job as soon as possible?...........	96	8.3%	108	11.2%
Missing/Not sure..............................	342	29.5%	186	19.0%

The high proportions of students, especially in Year 7, opting for 'not sure' make it very difficult to interpret their responses to this question. Although the increase in the proportion intending to get a job as soon as possible (8 per cent in Year 7 and 11 per cent in Year 9) is quite small, the increase in the proportions intending to 'go to another school or college' (26 per cent in Year 7 and 37 per cent in Year 9) is much greater: about 11 percentage points. This suggests that the Year 9 students may be less positively disposed towards their own schools than those in Year 7. It is, of course, possible that students may change their minds before the end of Year 11.

4.4.2 Students' behaviour in school

The questions shown in Tables 4.13 to 4.16 focused on students' behaviour in school.

Table 4.13   Students' behaviour in school this year: the responses of Year 7 and Year 9 students

	Year group			
	Year 7		Year 9	
Total...	1160	100.0%	980	100.0%
Describe your behaviour in class and around school this year .				
Always well behaved.........................	176	15.1%	178	18.2%
Usually well behaved.........................	763	65.8%	580	59.2%
Sometimes badly behaved................	188	16.2%	165	16.8%
Often badly behaved.........................	28	2.4%	20	2.1%
Missing..	6	.5%	37	3.7%
How often have you had punishments this year?				
Never..	444	38.3%	290	29.5%
Once or twice....................................	622	53.6%	531	54.2%
Quite often.......................................	58	5.0%	111	11.3%
Often..	30	2.6%	32	3.3%
Missing..	5	.5%	17	1.7%
Have you ever played truant this year?				
Yes..	100	8.6%	225	23.0%
No..	1051	90.6%	736	75.1%
Missing..	8	.7%	19	1.9%

The majority (about 80 per cent) of students in both age groups described themselves as always or usually well behaved in class and around school this year and there were no differences between the responses of the two groups (Table 4.13). However, the retrospective responses of the Year 9 students (Table 4.14) suggest that they remembered being slightly better behaved in Year 7 than they were now (38 per cent of the Year 9 students said that they were always well behaved in Year 7 compared with only 18 per cent in the current year).

**Table 4.14   Students' behaviour in school this and previous years:
current and retrospective responses of Year 9 students**

	This year Year 9		Last year Year 8		2 yrs. ago Year 7	
Total..	980	100.0%	980	100.0%	980	100.0%
Describe your behaviour in class and around school this year.						
Always well behaved...................	178	18.2%	192	19.6%	371	37.8%
Usually well behaved...................	580	59.2%	560	57.2%	399	40.7%
Sometimes badly behaved...........	165	16.8%	156	15.9%	95	9.7%
Often badly behaved....................	20	2.1%	30	3.0%	45	4.6%
Missing...	37	3.7%	42	4.3%	71	7.2%
How often have you had punishments this year?						
Never..	290	29.5%	275	28.1%	464	47.3%
Once or twice..............................	531	54.2%	539	55.0%	350	35.7%
Quite often..................................	111	11.3%	84	8.5%	62	6.4%
Often..	32	3.3%	32	3.2%	32	3.3%
Missing...	17	1.7%	50	5.1%	72	7.3%
Have you ever played truant this year?						
Yes..	225	23.0%	165	16.8%	112	11.4%
No..	736	75.1%	763	77.8%	787	80.3%
Missing...	19	1.9%	53	5.4%	81	8.3%

Table 4.13 shows that the Year 9 students were more likely than those in Year 7 to report having been given punishments (69 per cent, compared with only 61 per cent of those in Year 7). Although, in most cases, punishments had been given only 'once or twice', 14 per cent of the Year 9 students and 8 per cent of those in Year 7 reported receiving punishments often or quite often. The retrospective responses of the Year 9 students shown in Table 4.14, confirm that they had received fewer punishments when they were in Year 7.

Table 4.13 also shows that the responses of the Year 9 students with respect to their behaviour and frequency of punishment when they were in Year 8 were similar to their responses for the current year, whereas their responses for Year 7 suggest that they perceived themselves to have been better behaved and to have received fewer punishments in Year 7. This provides further support for the Working Group's hypothesis set out in Chapter 1.

Table 4.15   Frequency of truancy: the response of students who indicated they had played truant

	Year group			
	Year 7		Year 9	
Total indicating truancy this year.	100	100.0%	225	100.0%
A lesson here and there....................	29	29.0%	83	36.9%
A day here and there........................	58	58.0%	104	46.2%
Several days at a time......................	1	1.0%	10	4.4%
Weeks at a time...............................	4	4.0%	6	2.7%
Missing..	8	8.0%	22	9.8%
Total indicating truancy last year (when in Year 8).			165	100%
A lesson here and there....................	..	..	48	29.1%
A day here and there........................	..	..	84	50.9%
Several days at a time......................	..	..	9	5.5%
Weeks at a time...............................	..	..	2	1.2%
Missing..	..	..	22	13.3%
Total indicating truancy two years ago (when in Year 7).			112	100%
A lesson here and there....................	..	..	26	23.2%
A day here and there........................	..	..	57	50.9%
Several days at a time......................	..	..	7	6.3%
Weeks at a time...............................	..	..	3	2.7%
Missing..	..	..	19	17.0%

The percentages in this table are based on the numbers of students indicating that they had played truant in the relevant school year

One of the most striking findings of the study concerns the students' responses on truancy. The Year 9 students were far more likely than those in Year 7 to report having played truant. Nearly a quarter (23 per cent), compared with only 9 per cent of Year 7 students indicated that they had played truant this year (Table 4.13). In most cases, truanting students reported 'bunking off' either for 'a day here and there' or 'a lesson here and there' (Table 4.15). The retrospective responses of the Year 9 students also show an increase in the incidence of truancy from 11 per cent in Year 7 and 17 per cent in Year 8 to 23 per cent in Year 9 (Table 4.14).

Table 4.16   Bullying: the responses of Year 7 and Year 9 students

	Year group			
	Year 7		Year 9	
Total...	1160	100.0%	980	100.0%
Have you ever been bullied in school - this year?				
Never...	490	42.3%	651	66.4%
Once or twice.................................	495	42.7%	234	23.9%
Quite often....................................	100	8.6%	43	4.4%
Often...	71	6.1%	36	3.6%
Missing..	4	.3%	16	1.7%
Have you ever been bullied in school - last year?				
Never...	..	..	585	59.7%
Once or twice.................................	..	..	257	26.3%
Quite often....................................	..	..	59	6.0%
Often...	..	..	36	3.7%
Missing..	..	..	42	4.3%
Have you ever been bullied in school - in Year 7?				
Never...	..	..	568	57.9%
Once or twice.................................	..	..	239	24.4%
Quite often....................................	..	..	56	5.7%
Often...	..	..	46	4.7%
Missing..	..	..	71	7.3%

Although it is likely that students' definitions of bullying varied, the reported incidence of bullying was quite high, particularly amongst the Year 7 students (Table 4.16). More than half (57 per cent) of the Year 7 students, compared with about a third (32 per cent) of those in Year 9, reported being bullied in school this year. In most cases, this was reported as happening 'once or twice'. However, the difference between the two age groups could be a result of different definitions of bullying, since the retrospective responses of the Year 9 students showed very little difference in the amount of bullying reported for Years 7,8 or 9. It could be that Year 9 students have a 'tougher' definition of bullying. Nevertheless, it is worrying to note that 8 per cent of Year 9 students and 15 per cent of those in Year 7 reported being bullied often or quite often. Clearly more research is needed into bullying.

4.4.3 Students' activities in and out of school

The table below shows students' responses to questions concerning their activities in and out of school.

Table 4.17 Students' activities in and out of school: the responses of Year 7 and Year 9 students

	Year group			
	Year 7		Year 9	
Total....................................	1160	100.0%	980	100.0%
Do you take part in any lunchtime or after school activities?				
Yes.....................................	710	61.2%	519	53.0%
No......................................	369	31.8%	384	39.2%
Missing..............................	35	3.0%	29	3.0%
No activities in school...........	46	4.0%	48	4.8%
How many hours per day do you spend doing homework?				
I am not usually given homework...........	47	4.1%	57	5.8%
I am given homework but I do not do it...	23	2.0%	53	5.4%
Half hour or less................................	270	23.3%	195	19.9%
About 1 hour......................................	399	34.4%	264	26.9%
About 1 and half hours......................	211	18.2%	201	20.5%
About 2 hours....................................	94	8.1%	87	8.8%
About 2 and half hours......................	45	3.9%	52	5.3%
3 hours or more.................................	31	2.6%	19	2.0%
Missing..	39	3.4%	52	5.3%
Homework is important in helping me to do well at school.				
Strongly agree...................................	422	36.3%	214	21.9%
Agree...	522	45.0%	541	55.2%
Not sure..	81	7.0%	72	7.3%
Disagree..	94	8.1%	109	11.1%
Strongly disagree..............................	37	3.2%	34	3.5%
Missing..	4	.4%	10	1.0%
How often do you read on your own for fun outside school?				
(almost) every day.............................	462	39.9%	374	38.1%
once or twice a week..........................	350	30.2%	249	25.4%
once or twice a month........................	135	11.6%	157	16.0%
never or hardly ever...........................	205	17.6%	187	19.1%
Missing..	8	.7%	13	1.3%
How many hours each day do you watch TV or videos?				
0-1 hours...	175	15.1%	139	14.2%
about 2 hours.....................................	300	25.9%	274	28.0%
about 3 hours.....................................	292	25.1%	235	24.0%
about 4 hours.....................................	180	15.5%	162	16.5%
about 5 hours.....................................	92	8.0%	72	7.4%
6 hours or more..................................	102	8.8%	68	6.9%
Missing..	18	1.6%	28	2.9%

Although there were no differences between the schools of the Year 7 and Year 9 students in terms of the provision of lunchtime or after-school activities, more of the Year 7 students (61 per cent, compared with 53 per cent of the Year 9 students) reported taking part in such activities (Table 4.17).

Perhaps unexpectedly, there was very little difference in the amount of time the two age groups spent doing homework. Very approximately: about 10 per cent said they did not do homework; 20 per cent indicated that they spent half an hour a day or less; 30 per cent said they spent about an hour a day; 20 per cent, an hour and a half; and about 15 per cent two hours or more; about 5 per cent did not respond to this question. However, the majority of the students (81 per cent of those in Year 7 and 77 per cent of those in Year 9) strongly agreed or agreed that homework was important in helping them to do well at school' (Table 4.17). Once again, the responses of the Year 7 students were more positive than those of the Year 9 students.

The Year 7 students were more likely than those in Year 9 to report reading for pleasure outside school (70 per cent reported doing so at least once or twice a week, compared with only 64 per cent of the Year 9 students). Although the proportions reading for fun every day were very similar, some five per cent fewer Year 9 students reported reading for fun once or twice a week . It may simply be that, unless they were very keen readers, Year 9 students felt that they had less time than those in Year 7 to spend on reading. It is also interesting to note that nearly one fifth (18 per cent of the Year 7 students and 19 per cent of those in Year 9) said that they never or hardly ever read for fun outside school.

Interestingly, there was no difference in the amount of time the two age groups reported spending watching television or videos. Just over 40 per cent of the students spent two hours or less each day watching television or videos, one quarter spent three hours, and nearly a third watched for four hours or more each day (Table 4.17).

4.5   Parents' attitudes to school and education

There were a number of statements and questions in the questionnaire concerned with students' perceptions of their parents' attitudes to school and education. These fell into two main groups: those concerned with their parents' views on the value of education; and those concerned with parental interest and support.

4.5.1   Parents' opinions about the value of education

The questionnaire included two statements relating to the students' perceptions of their parents' opinions about the value of education. These are shown in Table 4.18

Table 4.18 Parents' opinions about the value of education:
the views of Year 7 and Year 9 students

	Year group			
	Year 7		Year 9	
Total.................................	1160	100.0%	980	100.0%
My parents think it is important for me to do well at school.				
Strongly agree............................	887	76.5%	664	67.7%
Agree...	240	20.7%	291	29.7%
Not sure..	15	1.3%	9	1.0%
Disagree..	2	.2%	5	.6%
Strongly disagree...........................	5	.4%	4	.4%
Missing/not sure...........................	11	.9%	7	.7%
My parents think school is a waste of time.				
Strongly agree...............................	7	.6%	7	.7%
Agree...	6	.5%	4	.4%
Not sure..	26	2.2%	12	1.2%
Disagree..	133	11.4%	152	15.5%
Strongly disagree...........................	982	84.7%	799	81.5%
Missing...	7	.6%	6	.6%

There were no differences in the overall proportions of Year 7 and Year 9 students responding positively to this set of statements (Table 4.18). Almost all (97 per cent of both age groups) strongly agreed or agreed that their parents thought it was important for them to do well at school, and 97 per cent of both groups disagreed with the statement that their parents thought school was a waste of time.

However, it should be noted that the Year 7 students were more likely than those in Year 9 to select the most positive response options (i.e. 'strongly agree') when responding to the first of these statements.

4.5.2 Parental interest and support

The research reported in Part II of this report showed that lack of parental interest and support were related to early leaving and dropout (Part II, Sections 2.2 and 4.2). A number of statements and questions concerned with parental interest and support were, therefore, included in the questionnaire. These are shown in Table 4.19. It is important to note that both age groups indicated a high level of parental support and interest.

Table 4.19   Parental interest and support: the views of Year 7 and Year 9 students

	Year group			
	Year 7		Year 9	
Total..	1160	100.0%	980	100.0%
What do you think that your parents want you to do?				
Go on to univ/poly/other college	744	64.2%	624	63.7%
Get a job as soon as possible.............	107	9.2%	104	10.6%
Missing/not sure................................	309	26.6%	252	25.7%
My parents are interested in how I do at school.				
Always...	916	78.9%	679	69.3%
Nearly always....................................	171	14.8%	188	19.2%
Sometimes...	53	4.6%	88	9.0%
Hardly ever.......................................	11	.9%	12	1.2%
Never..	3	.3%	2	.2%
Missing...	6	.5%	12	1.2%
My parents come to school parents' evenings.				
Always...	701	60.4%	563	57.4%
Nearly always....................................	247	21.3%	189	19.3%
Sometimes...	144	12.4%	121	12.4%
Hardly ever.......................................	33	2.8%	61	6.2%
Never..	29	2.5%	40	4.1%
Missing...	6	.6%	6	.6%
My parents make it clear that I should behave well in school.				
Strongly agree....................................	520	44.8%	343	35.0%
Agree..	525	45.2%	514	52.4%
Not sure..	54	4.7%	51	5.2%
Disagree..	43	3.7%	56	5.7%
Strongly disagree...............................	6	.5%	10	1.0%
Missing...	12	1.1%	5	.6%
My parents make sure I do my homework.				
Always...	750	64.7%	394	40.2%
Nearly always....................................	254	21.9%	298	30.4%
Sometimes...	108	9.3%	164	16.7%
Hardly ever.......................................	28	2.4%	78	7.9%
Never..	15	1.3%	39	4.0%
Missing...	5	.4%	8	.8%
Do you talk to your parents about your career plans?				
Often..	346	29.8%	440	44.9%
Sometimes...	556	47.9%	432	44.1%
Never or hardly..................................	152	13.1%	67	6.8%
Missing...	106	9.2%	41	4.1%

There were no differences between the two age groups in their perceptions of what their parents wanted them to do after they had left school. Nearly two-thirds of both groups believed that their parents wanted them to go on to a university, polytechnic or other college.

However, on the other statements concerned with parental interest, attendance at parents' evenings, encouragement of good behaviour and making sure that homework was done, there was a consistent pattern of slightly more positive response from the Year 7 students. For example 94 per cent of the Year 7 students compared with 89 per cent of those in Year 9 indicated that their parents were always or nearly always interested in how they did at school and 82 per cent compared with 77 per cent reported that their parents always or nearly always came to parents' evenings. Once again, the younger age group were more likely to select the most positive option ('strongly agree').

Perhaps not surprisingly, the older age group (Year 9) were more likely to have talked often to their parents about their career plans (45 per cent reported doing so often and 44 per cent sometimes). These proportions are much higher than those reporting discussing career plans with teachers (Table 4.9).

4.5.3   Talking to other family members and friends about career plans

Our review of the literature identified several studies showing that the peer group can play an important part in shaping young people's attitudes, beliefs and behaviour (Part II, Section 4.1.2). A number of statements concerned with discussing career plans with family members other than parents or friends were, therefore, included in the questionnaire. These are shown in Table 4.20

About 25 per cent of the Year 9 students reported discussing their career plans with their friends often and 54 per cent sometimes. Not unexpectedly, the Year 9 students were more likely than those in Year 7 to discuss their career plans with their friends. Rather fewer students in both age groups reported discussing career plans with siblings or other family members, but the differential between Year 9 and Year 7 remained.

Table 4.20   Talking to other family members and friends about career plans: the responses of Year 7 and Year 9 students

	Year group			
	Year 7		Year 9	
Total..	1160	100.0%	980	100.0%
Do you talk to your friends about your career plans?				
Often..	171	14.7%	246	25.1%
Sometimes...	517	44.5%	530	54.1%
Never or hardly..................................	233	20.0%	116	11.9%
Missing..	240	20.7%	87	8.9%
Do you talk to other family members about career plans?				
Often..	91	7.8%	84	8.5%
Sometimes...	363	31.3%	368	37.5%
Never or hardly..................................	406	35.0%	395	40.3%
Missing..	300	25.9%	134	13.7%
Do you talk to brothers or sisters about your career plans?				
Often..	98	8.4%	95	9.6%
Sometimes...	263	22.7%	306	31.2%
Never or hardly..................................	494	42.6%	433	44.2%
Missing..	306	26.4%	146	14.9%

4.6 Summary

The comparisons described in this chapter support the hypothesis set out in Chapter 1 that the attitudes towards school and learning of Year 7 students are more positive than those of students in Year 9. Nevertheless, it is important to note that the majority of students in both age groups expressed favourable attitudes on most of the topics covered in the questionnaire, and that the differences between the two age groups were greater on some issues than on others. It is also important to bear in mind that some of the differences between the two age groups (particularly the less frequent selection of 'strongly agree' by the Year 9 students) may be because they are becoming more mature, discerning and worldly wise and thus more selective in their views of the world around them. The main findings are summarised below.

4.6.1.   Attitudes towards school and school work

i.   The responses of the Year 7 students to most of the statements concerned with their attitudes towards school and school work tended to be more favourable than those of the Year 9 students. In particular, Year 7 students were more likely than those in Year 9 to agree that school work was interesting and less likely to indicate that lessons were boring.

ii.   The majority of students in both age groups (around 90 per cent) expressed very positive attitudes towards the value of school and learning. Slightly fewer (60-75 per cent, depending on question) responded positively towards statements concerned with liking school. Their responses to statements concerned with interest and boredom were even less positive: only about 60 per cent of all students found their work interesting in all or most lessons and minorities of both age groups perceived all or most of their lessons to be boring.

iii.   The vast majority of the students in both age groups held strong views on the 'utilitarian' purposes of school. They believed that schools should help them to do well in exams, teach them things which would be useful when they got jobs and to be independent. There were no differences between the responses of the two age groups on these issues. However, slightly fewer of the Year 9 students (84 per cent compared with 89 per cent of those in Year 7) were convinced that school work would help them get a job.

iv.   The students' open-ended comments revealed that the most important ways they thought their schools could help them prepare for their future were (in descending order of frequency) by: helping them to acquire life skills; supporting and encouraging them; providing knowledge about careers: providing them with high-quality education; helping them to gain qualifications for further study or in order to get a job.

4.6.2 Teachers, teaching and the maintenance of discipline

i.   The Year 7 students were more likely than those in Year 9 to say that they liked all or most of their teachers (60 per cent and 40 per cent, respectively, agreed with this statement).

ii.   The Year 7 students held more positive perceptions of their teachers' efforts to ensure the quality of their work. However, more than a quarter of the Year 9 students and nearly one fifth of those in Year 7 said that their teachers 'were fairly easily satisfied' with their work.

iii.   There is evidence that many teachers did not praise their students for good work. Only 58 per cent of the Year 7 students and 50 per cent of those in Year 9 indicated that all or most of their teachers praised them when they did their work well.

iv.   Year 7 students were more likely to perceive that their teachers were making efforts to maintain discipline and far more likely to agree that all or most of their teachers could keep order in class (76 per cent of the Year 7 students compared with only 56 per cent of those in Year 9 agreed that all or most of their teachers could keep order in class).

v.   There was also evidence that many students did not discuss their work individually with their teachers. Over 40 per cent of the Year 7 and Year 9 students said that they never or hardly ever talked to their teachers on their own about their work.

vi.   Not unexpectedly, in view of their age, the Year 9 students were more likely than those in Year 7 to have talked to teachers about their career plans. However, over 50 per cent of the Year 9 students said they never or hardly ever talked to their teachers about their career plans.

vii.   Both age groups expressed the greatest preference for lessons where they could work with their friends and the lowest preference for lessons where they worked alone.

4.6.3 Students' behaviour in school and out-of-school activities

i.　There were no statistically significant differences between the Year 7 and Year 9 samples of students in terms of perceived ability. However, the Year 7 students were more likely than those in Year 9 to say that they worked hard in their lessons.

ii.　The majority of students described themselves as always or usually well behaved in class and around school. There were no differences between the responses of the two age groups. However, in their retrospective responses, the Year 9 students revealed a slight decrease in their standards of behaviour since Year 7.

iii.　The Year 9 students were more likely than those in Year 7 to report having been given punishments and their retrospective responses indicated that they had received fewer punishments in previous years.

iv.　An important finding of this study was that the Year 9 students were far more likely than those in Year 7 to report having played truant, most commonly for a day or a lesson 'here and there' (23 per cent of those in Year 9, compared with only nine per cent in Year 7). The retrospective responses of the Year 9 students showed a progressive increase in the incidence of truancy between Year 7 and Year 9.

v.　Another important finding concerns the extent of bullying reported by the students. Although it is likely that students' definitions of bullying varied, the reported incidence of bullying was quite high, particularly amongst the Year 7 students. More than half of the Year 7 students and about a third of those in Year 9 reported being bullied in school this year. In most cases, this was reported as happening 'once or twice'. However, 8 per cent of Year 9 students and 15 per cent of those in Year 7 reported being bullied often or quite often.

vi.　A higher proportion of the Year 7 students (66 per cent, compared with 58 per cent of the Year 9 students) reported taking part in lunch time and after-school activities.

vii.　Very little difference was found in the time spent on homework by the two age groups. The majority reported spending between half an hour and one-and-a-half hours a day on homework.

viii.　There was no difference in the amount of time the two age groups reported spending watching television or videos. Just over 40 per cent of the students spent two hours or less each day watching television or videos, one quarter spent three hours, and one third watched for four hours or more each day.

4.6.4 Parents' attitudes to school and education

i.   Both age groups indicated a high level of parental support and interest in school and education (in terms of attendance at parents' evenings, encouragement of good behaviour). However, the responses of the Year 7 students were slightly more positive than those of the Year 9 students.

ii. There were no differences between the two age groups in their perceptions of what their parents wanted them to do after they had left school. Nearly two thirds of the students reported that their parents wanted them to go on to a college, polytechnic or university after leaving school.

iii. Perhaps not surprisingly, the older age group (Year 9) were more likely to have talked to their parents about their career plans.

iv. Both groups of students reported talking about career plans more frequently with parents, friends and siblings than with teachers.

CHAPTER 5
FACTORS ASSOCIATED WITH MOTIVATION TOWARDS SCHOOL AND LEARNING

5.1 Introduction

The purpose of this chapter is to fulfil the second aim of the research outlined in Chapter 1:

- to identify the factors associated with motivation towards school and hypothesise causes for hostility towards school.

This chapter describes the results of the correlation and multilevel regression analyses, which are set out in detail in Appendices 2 and 3, concerning the associations between students' motivation towards school and a range of school, student and home background factors, and compares the relative strengths of these relationships. The results of these analyses are described under the following main headings:

- the selection of an outcome measure to reflect students' attitudes towards school and learning;
- the input measures selected for inclusion in the analyses;
- the results of the correlation and regression analyses.

5.2 The selection of an outcome measure

In order to identify the home and school factors associated with students' motivation towards school, it was necessary to develop or identify a variable or scale which could be regarded as a surrogate measure for students' motivation towards school, and thus act as our output measure.

There are several advantages in using a scale made up of a number of variables, rather than an individual item, such as 'On the whole, I like being at school', to reflect students' motivation towards school and learning. A scale is more likely to provide a reliable measure of an individual student's attitude towards school since it includes information on his or her attitudes towards several different aspects of school (such as everyday life in school, school work and teachers), whereas an individual item can only focus on a single aspect. A student who is truly hostile towards school is likely to be hostile to many aspects of school. Furthermore, the inclusion in a scale of positive and negative items focusing on the same issue (for example 'School work is worth doing' and 'The work I do in lessons is a waste of time') is likely to make the scale more reliable, since students are forced to consider their attitudes towards a particular aspect of school in contrasting ways.

We selected as our surrogate for students' motivation towards school, a composite measure, the Positive Attitudes Towards School Scale (Table 5.1), made up of ten statements from the student questionnaire,which appeared to:

- reflect those aspects of students' attitudes towards school and schooling which have been shown by previous research (Part II, Sections 4.3.1 and 4.3.2) to be associated with motivation towards school: liking for school; interest versus boredom with school; perceived value of school and school work; like/dislike of teachers;

- form a distinct group in the factor analyses described in Appendix 2 (i.e. they correlated fairly strongly with each other).

Scores of this scale were computed by summing a student's scores on each contributory item (after reversing the scoring of negative items). A high score on the scale meant that a student had a positive attitude towards school and a low score indicated a negative attitude. The items forming the Positive Attitudes Towards School Scale, and its component dimensions (the Sub-scales), are shown in Table 5.1.

Table 5.1 The Positive Attitudes Towards School Scale

Liking for School Sub-scale:
>> I am very happy when I am at school.
>> On the whole I like being at school.
>> Most of the time I don't want to go to school.

Interest versus Boredom Sub-scale:
>> The work I do in lessons is interesting to me.
>> I am bored in lessons.
>> In a lesson I often count the minutes till it ends.

Value of School Sub-scale:
>> School work is worth doing.
>> The work I do in lessons is a waste of time.
>> School is a waste of time for me.

Liking for Teachers Sub-scale:
>> I like my teachers.

5.3 The input measures

The other scales and items included in the correlation and regression analyses fell into three broad groups: home measures; school measures and student measures. These are summarised below and described in more detail in Appendix 2.

5.3.1 Home measures

The home measures used in the analyses included a surrogate measure for the cultural level of the home (the number of books in the home) and four variables concerned with students' perceptions of their parents' involvement and support (interest in how well their child does at school, attendance at parents' evenings, educational aspirations and discussion of career plans).

5.3.2 School measures

The school measures used in the analyses included a number of background variables (type of catchment area, type of school, percentage of students receiving free school meals, percentage of students from ethnic minorities, reading age of intake, GCSE results, and procedures used to review/monitor students' progress) and year group.

5.3.3 Student measures

The student measures used in the analyses included three measures concerned with students' perceptions of school (the Positive School Ethos Scale, the Utilitarian Purposes of School Scale, the Talking Individually with Teachers Scale), a scale concerned with perceived ability and perseverance, three items concerned with behaviour (frequency of punishments, frequency of truancy, and time spent on homework), whether or not the student intended to remain in education post-16, and sex.

5.4 The results of the correlation and regression analyses

The results described in this section are discussed in greater detail in Appendix 3, which also gives information on the statistical procedures used in the analyses.

5.4.1 Technical details

This section is included in order to explain the rationale behind the correlation and regression analyses. Readers without a statistical background may prefer to go directly to Section 5.4.2.

The simple correlations in Table A3.2 in Appendix 3 provide evidence about the strength of the links between the component sub-scales (or dimensions) of the Positive Attitudes Towards School Scale.

The simple correlations shown in Table A3.3, on the other hand, provide an indication of the strength of the relationships between our outcome measure (the Positive Attitudes Towards School Scale) and each of the other variables included in the analyses (the input measures) before taking account of their intercorrelations with each other.

Tables A3.4 to A3.5 take us further towards an explanation of students' liking for and hostility towards school. These tables contain information which identifies the input variables which are most likely to be important in explaining differences between students' in their attitudes towards school once the intercorrelations between input variables have been taken into account.

Because year group and school sample are confounded in our research design, (i.e. all the Year 7 students were in Sample A school and all the Year 9 students were in Sample B schools (see Chapters 2 and 3)), there remains the possibility that other school-level factors could account for the observed statistically significant differences between year groups. To investigate this, we carried out a multilevel analysis with the Positive Attitudes to School Scale as the dependent variable in which we included both the year group factor, and other school-level variables. Results were reassuring: the year group effect remained substantial and statistically significant, while, with only one exception, none of the other school-level variables achieved statistical significance (Table A 3.4).

The final multilevel analyses shown in Table A3.6 are based on the assumption that the input measures are chronologically related to each other in the life of the student as follows:

• home measures

• school measures

• students' perceptions of and behaviour in school

and that, as Peaker (1971) argued, 'earlier events can influence later events...and consequently the apparent influence of the late events on still later ones should be discounted by what is known about the earlier events'. The input measures were, therefore, entered 'stepwise' into the analysis in the order: home; school; students' perceptions and behaviour. Thus, for example, any variations which could be explained either by home measures or school measures are deemed to be explained by home measures on the grounds that the home pre-existed the school in the life of the student.

5.4.2 The various aspects of students' attitudes towards school

Table A3.2 in Appendix 3 shows that there were moderate to strong statistically significant positive correlations between the Liking for School Sub-scale and the other three component sub-scales of the Positive Attitudes Towards School Scale, which ranged from 0.45 - 0.58. These results, which are consistent with the previous research described in Part II, Sections 4.3.1 and 4.3.2, suggests that:

Students who like school tend to:

- be interested in school work

- think school and school work are important

- like their teachers.

Students who are hostile towards school tend to:

- be bored by school work

- think school and school work are unimportant

- dislike their teachers.

5.4.3 Home measures and their associations with students' attitudes towards school

The previous research reported in Part II of this report suggests that the associations between socio-economic status and students' motivation towards education is not strong (Part II, Section 4.2.1). However, there is evidence from previous research which links parental support with positive attitudes and staying on at school (Part II, Section 4.2.2).

Our surrogate measure for the cultural level of the home (number of books in the home) was found to have very low simple correlations (0.08 - 0.09) with the Positive Attitudes Towards School Scale for both year groups (Table A3.3) and was not signficantly associated with it in the multilevel regression analyses (Tables A3.4 - A3.6), ie this measure was not a significant factor in explaining variations in students' attitudes towards school. However, it should be borne in mind that this measure can only give a very approximate indication of cultural level.

On the other hand, the three measures concerned with perceived parental interest and support were found to have slightly higher simple correlations (0.17 - 0.26) with our output measure (Table A3.3) and in our stepwise multilevel regression analyses (Table A3.6) the parental support group of measures was found to explain 10 - 13 per cent of the variation in students' attitudes towards school.

5.4.4 School measures and their associations with students' attitudes towards school

The majority of the school background measures derived from the school questionnaire appeared to be almost unrelated to the Positive Attitudes Towards School Scale for either age group: only nine of the 30 simple correlations reported achieved statistical significance and only two were greater than 0.10. (Table A3.3)

For this reason, only three of these measures (school type; metropolitan/non-metropolitan LEA; school monitoring and recording procedures) were included in the multilevel regression analyses. Although one of these measures, the type of monitoring and recording procedures used, was found to be significantly associated with students' attitudes towards school when both year groups were combined (ie when the sample size was doubled), no associations were found between school catchment measures and students' attitudes towards school when the year groups were analysed separately.

As expected, in view of the findings described in the previous chapter, year group was found to be a significant predictor of students' attitudes towards school (Table A3.4) (ie Year 7 students were likely to hold more positive attitudes towards school than were those in Year 9.).

The Positive School Ethos Scale, which reflected students' perceptions of their school's ethos or climate (a high score on this scale indicated that the student thought his or her school had a good reputation, well-maintained premises, clear rules of behaviour and firm discipline, and good teaching practices, such as frequent praise, high expectations and regular marking) was found to have moderately strong simple correlations (0.43 and 0.40) with our outcome measure (Table A3.3), to be significantly associated with it (Table A3.5) and to explain 8 - 12 per cent of the variation in students' attitudes towards school (Table A3.6).

Similarly, the Utilitarian Purposes of School scale, which indicated the strength of students' own belief (and their perceptions of their parents' belief) that schools should help students to do well in examinations, prepare them for jobs and help them become independent, was found to have moderately strong correlations (0.39 and 0.38) with our outcome measure and to be significantly associated with it (Table A3.5). However, in the multilevel regression analyses shown in Table A3.6, probably because of its correlation with some of the parental support measures entered earlier in the analysis (Appendix 3 and Section 5.4.1), it was found to explain only about three to four per cent of the variation in students' attitudes towards school.

One further school measure, the scale concerned with talking individually with teachers, which was derived from the student questionnaire, was found to be have low but significant positive correlations with the Positive Attitudes Towards School Scale (Table A3.3) and to be unassociated with our outcome measure in the multilevel regression analyses (Tables A3.4 - A3.6). This is probably because this measure was positively correlated with some of the parental involvement measures and with the Positive School Ethos Scale, all of which were entered earlier in the analysis (Appendix 3 and Section 5.4.1).

5.4.5 Student measures and their associations with students' attitudes towards school

The results shown in Tables A3.3 to A3.6 suggest that girls tend to have slightly more positive attitudes towards school than do boys. However, the difference does not appear to be very great and sex was only found to explain about one per cent of the variation in students' attitudes towards school (Table A3.6).

On the other hand, the Perceived Ability and Perseverance scale showed moderately strong (0.41 and 0.42) simple correlations with the Positive Attitudes Towards School Scale (Table A3.3), was significantly associated with it (Table A3.5) and was found to explain five to six per cent of the variation in students' attitudes for school (Table A3.6), ie students who see themselves as able and hard-working tend to hold positive attitudes towards school.

The three measures concerned with students' behaviour (infrequency of punishment, frequency of truancy and time spent doing homework) were found to have low to moderate correlations (negative in the case of truancy) with our outcome measure, to be significantly associated with it (Table A3.5) and to explain about four per cent of the variation in students' attitudes towards school (Table A3.6). This is consistent with the previous research reported (Part II, Section 2.2) which also found links between attitudes towards school and behaviour.

Finally, students' own educational aspirations (in terms of their intention to remain in education post-16) were found to have low positive correlations with our outcome measure (Table A3.3), to be significantly associated with it (Table A3.5) and to explain about one per cent of the variation in students' attitudes towards school (Table A5.6).

Altogether, the home, school and student input measures included in the multilevel regression analyses explained about 36 per cent of the variation in students' attitudes towards school.

5.5   Summary

5.5.1   *The various dimensions of students' attitudes towards school*

i   Students who like school tend to be interested in school work, think school and school work are important and to like their teachers.

ii   Students who are hostile towards school tend to be bored by school work, think school and school work are unimportant and to dislike their teachers.

5.5.2   *The home and parental support*

i   The parental support and interest measures explained 10 - 13 per cent of the variation in students' attitudes towards school.

ii   Our surrogate measure for the cultural level of the home only explained about one per cent of the variation in students' attitudes towards school.

5.5.3   *The school*

i   The school catchment area and intake measures used, in our analyses, were not strongly correlated with students' attitudes towards school.

ii   The analyses described in this chapter confirm the findings outlined in Chapter 4: Year 7 students were likely to hold more positive attitudes towards school than were students in Year 9.

iii   Our results suggest that students with positive attitudes towards school tend to perceive the ethos of their schools to be positive (a good reputation, well-maintained premises, clear rules of behaviour and firm discipline, and good teaching practices, such as frequent praise, high expectations and regular marking). The Positive School Ethos Scale explained 8 - 12 per cent of the variation in students' attitudes towards school.

iv   Our findings also suggest that students with positive attitudes towards school tend to believe that schools should help students to do well in examinations, prepare them for jobs, and help them become independent (and to believe that their parents held similar views). The Utilitarian Purposes of School Scale explained three to four per cent of the variation in students' attitudes towards school.

5.5.4 The students

i   Our results suggest that students who have positive attitudes towards school tend to see themselves as hard-working, high-achieving and well-regarded by their teachers. The Perceived Ability and Perseverance Scale explained about five to six per cent of the variation on students' attitudes towards school.

ii   Our findings also suggest that such students tend to be well-behaved, unlikely to truant, and likely to spend longer on their homework. The student behavioural measures explained about four per cent of the variation in students' attitudes towards school.

iii   There was also a slight tendency for girls to have more positive attitudes towards school than boys and for high academic aspirations to be associated with positive attitudes towards school. However, each of these measures explained only about one per cent of the variation in students' attitudes towards school.

CHAPTER 6

OVERVIEW AND CONCLUSIONS

6.1. Introduction

The research described in this report was undertaken by the National Foundation for Educational Research on behalf of the Working Group on Schools, Society and Citizenship of the National Commission on Education. Appendix 1 gives brief information on the commission, its membership and its work.

The main aims of the study were to investigate the experiences and attitudes of 11-and 13-year-old students (Year 7 and 9) to their schools in order to:

- test the hypothesis that students' levels of motivation towards schooling are lower in Year 9 than in Year 7;

- identify the factors associated with motivation towards school and learning and hypothesise causes for hostility towards school;

- highlight those results which are most likely to assist the Commission's Working Party on Schools, Society and Citizenship in the formulation of its recommendations.

The research consisted of questionnaire surveys of students in Years 7 and 9 and their schools, complemented by a review of previous research (Part II of this report).

The main topics covered in the questionnaires for students were:

- personal and home background information;

- attitudes towards school and learning;

- perceptions of teachers and lessons;

- self-reported behaviour in and out of school;

- perceptions of parental interest and support.

The questionnaire for schools sought background information on catchment area, examination results and procedures used to support the progress of Key Stage 3 students.

Detailed summaries of the results of the research have been provided at the end of each chapter of this report. This concluding chapter, therefore, consists of an overview of some of the key findings of the study, together with an indication of their possible implications for the Working Group and others concerned with the quality of education.

6.2 Comparisons between the levels of motivation towards school and learning of students in Year 7 and Year 9

In general, the findings of this study support the hypothesis that students' levels of motivation towards schooling are lower in Year 9 than in Year 7. It is possible, of course, that some of the differences between the two age groups, especially where there appears to have been a shift from an extreme response by Year 7 students to a less extreme response by those in Year 9 (for example from 'strongly agree' to 'agree'), could have arisen from the fact that the older students have become more discerning and worldly wise and less willing to express extreme levels of enthusiasm. This caveat should be borne in mind when considering the following results. The most striking differences between the two age groups are given below.

Compared with Year 7 students, those in Year 9 were:

- less likely to say that their school work was interesting and more likely to say that their lessons were boring (Table 4.2);

- less likely to say that they liked all or most of their teachers (Table 4.6);

- less likely to agree that their teachers tried hard to make them work as well as they were able (Table 4.7);

- less likely to agree that their teachers were making efforts to maintain discipline (Table 4.8);

- less likely to agree that their teachers could keep order in class and that their school had sensible rules (Table 4.8);

- more likely to have played truant (23 per cent compared with only 9 per cent of those in Year 7) (Tables 4.14 and 4.15).

There was very little or no difference between the Year 7 and Year 9 samples of students in:

- their perceptions of their own ability, which were quite positive (Table 4.11);

- their strong belief that schools should help them to do well in exams, teach them things which would be useful when they got jobs and to be independent (Table 4.4);

- their perceptions of their parents' aspirations for their future (Table 4.19).

6.3 The factors associated with motivation towards school and learning

The correlation and regression analyses reported in Chapter 5 showed that the following factors were associated with positive attitudes towards school amongst Year 9 and Year 7 students:

- interest in school work (and lack of boredom);
- liking for teachers;
- a belief in the value of school and school work;
- positive perceptions of the school's ethos;
- positive views of their own ability and perseverance;
- good behaviour in school;
- a high level of perceived parental support.

These findings suggest that students who dislike school are more likely than those expressing more positive attitudes to:

- find school boring;
- dislike their teachers;
- place low values on school and schoolwork;
- have negative perceptions of the ethos of their school;
- have negative views of their own ability and perseverance;
- behave badly in school;
- perceive lower levels of support from their parents.

The following factors were found to be unassociated, or only weakly associated, with motivation towards school and learning:

- type of catchment area; type of school, the percentage of students receiving free school meals; reading age of intake, GCSE results; and retention rates;
- the cultural level of the home (although this finding should be regarded with caution since only one surrogate measure was included in the analysis).

Most of the conclusions of this study have been based on students' perceptions of their schools and their teachers, which may not, of course, always accurately reflect life in school. However, it should be borne in mind that students' perceptions of school and teachers are of paramount importance and are likely to be a major influence on their behaviour in school and attitudes towards education.

6.4   Other important findings of the research

There were a number of findings of the research which, although not directly related to the hypotheses set out at the beginning of this chapter, may well have implications for the work of the Commission.

It is important to bear in mind that:

- in spite of the age-related differences identified in Section 6.2, the majority of students in both age groups expressed favourable attitudes on most of the aspects of school covered in the questionnaire.

However, some of the other findings of the research give cause for concern.

- A fairly substantial minority of students said they found their school work boring (about 9 per cent indicated they were bored in all or most lessons and a further 40 - 55 per cent said that they were bored in some lessons) (Table 4.2).

- Many teachers did not praise their students for good work (only about half of the students said that all or most of their teachers praised them when they did good work) (Table 4.7).

- A substantial minority (nearly a quarter) of students perceived their teachers to be 'fairly easily satisfied' with their students' work (Table 4.7).

- Many students (about 40 per cent) said they had not discussed their work individually with their teachers during this school year (Table 4.9).

- Students in both age groups expressed the greatest preference for lessons where they could work with their friends and the least preference for lessons where they worked alone (Table 4.10).

- The majority of students perceived a high level of parental interest and support and both age groups reported talking about their career plans more frequently with their parents than with their teachers (Tables 4.19 and 4.9).

- The reported incidence of bullying appeared quite high, particularly amongst the Year 7 students. More than half of the Year 7 students and about a third of those in Year 9 reported being bullied in school during the current school year, although usually only 'once or twice'. However, 15 per cent of Year 7 students and 8 per cent of those in Year 9 reported being bullied 'often or quite often' (Table 4.16). Nevertheless, it must be stressed that students were not provided with, or asked for, a definition of bullying and that it seems inevitable that the definitions they used would have varied. For this reason, our findings with regard to bullying should be regarded with caution. It seems clear that further research into the incidence of bullying is needed.

- More than half the students in both age groups said that they spent three hours or more each day watching television or videos (Table 4.17).

6.5   The main implications of the research

This research has shown that students' attitudes towards school and learning tend to deteriorate to some extent as they progress from Year 7 to Year 9 in their secondary schools. Our findings also suggest that, although the majority of students expressed positive views about school and education, a minority appears to be disaffected.

Our regression analyses, however, identified a number of factors which were associated with positive attitudes towards school. Many of these have implications for teachers, school managers and the education system. The main implications of our study are, therefore, discussed under the following headings:

- Teaching and learning practices

- School management

- The education system as a whole

- Further research.

6.5.1   Teaching and learning practices

The study identified quite strong associations between students' attitudes and a range of aspects of teaching behaviour. High expectations on the part of the teacher, regular feedback, praise for good work and effective classroom discipline (all of which formed part of the 'Positive School Ethos' factor described in Chapter 5 and Appendix 2) were shown to be associated with students' positive attitudes towards school and education. This finding is not new. The previous research described in our review of the literature (Part II, Section 4.4), found similar results and most educationalists are aware of the importance of these factors. However, the results of our research suggest that many teachers were not lavish with praise, that a minority of teachers were 'fairly easily satisfied' and that many pupils did not talk individually with their teachers about their work. It seems clear that there is a need for action which will encourage and enable teachers to make more use of strategies, such as high expectations, regular feedback, and praise for good work, which this and other research has shown to be associated with students' positive attitudes towards school.

The research showed that substantial minorities of students found school work boring. It also found that students liked lessons where they could work with their friends and lessons where they could make things, and much preferred lessons where they had discussions to lessons where they worked alone. Strategies which involve students in their own learning and build upon their preferences for co-operative and practical work and discussions could well help to remotivate bored and disaffected students.

6.5.2   School management

Other factors found to be associated with positive attitudes on the part of students were related to the way their schools were managed: effective discipline; well-maintained premises; a good reputation; and well-behaved students. This result is also consistent with previous research. However, the results of our study on the extent of truancy and bullying, for example, suggest that a minority, at least, of schools may need to take action on these issues.

The results of this research also suggest that students believe strongly that schools should help them to pass examinations, teach them things that will help them when they get jobs and help them to become independent. Those involved in developing new curricula could well bear this finding in mind.

6.5.3   Beyond the school

The study found that parental interest and support were associated with positive attitudes towards education. Interestingly, most of the students taking part in this study believed that their parents were interested in their progress, supportive and held high aspirations. Yet there is a great deal of anecdotal evidence on the low level of parental involvement in secondary education. It may be that this results from parents' lack of confidence (Wedge and Prosser, 1973) and understanding of the educational process, rather than from a lack of interest. It seems clear that secondary schools in all types of catchment areas could, with advantage, consider the development or expansion of strategies designed to capitalise on the parental interest perceived by the students taking part in this study. Further investigation of some of the schemes developed in disadvantaged areas (Part II, Section 5) may provide useful ideas of ways in which parents could be involved more fully in their children's schooling. However, it should not be forgotten that such schemes, which could well involve home visiting and other out-of-school hours activities, are likely to require additional resources (not least in terms of staff time).

6.5.4.   Further research

The results of this study have raised a number of questions, many of which can only be answered by further research. It is particularly important to investigate the following issues more fully.

- As indicated in section 6.5.3 above, we found that students' perceptions of parental interest and support were associated with positive attitudes towards school, and previous research (Part II, Sections 2.2 and 4.2.2) has identified links between parental involvement and their children's achievement. Furthermore, one of the stated purposes of the Parents'

Charter is to help parents become more effective partners in their children's education. As far as we are aware, no baseline data exist on the current level of interest and involvement in their children's education amongst the totality of parents in England and Wales. Although the reforms initiated by the Education (No. 2) Act 1986 and the Education Reform Act 1988, giving parents greater power in the management of schools, have resulted in the greater involvement of some parents, there is anecdotal evidence from secondary school teachers that large numbers of parents show little interest or involvement in their children's education. The findings of our research, however, suggest that most Year 7 and Year 9 student believed that their parents were interested in their schooling. This suggests that there may be a pool of parental interest waiting to be tapped. The purpose of further research in this area would be to map the extent and type of parental involvement in their children's secondary schooling; identify parents' reasons for becoming or not becoming involved; identify those aspects of schooling which parents consider to be most important for their children's future; describe examples of good practice and make recommendations on ways in which secondary schools could involve parents more fully and effectively.

- Our study has provided a broad brush picture of the associations between certain teaching approaches (such as holding and expressing high expectations, regular feedback and ample praise) and students' positive attitudes towards school and learning. An in-depth research study designed to identify and describe examples of good classroom practice and incorporate these into staff development materials would be of great value to the education profession.

- A substantial minority of the students taking part in the study indicated that they believed they had been the subject of bullying. This study did not provide or ask for any definitions of bullying, and it could well be that many students included less serious behaviour under the general category of bullying. However, we cannot be sure that this is the case. Clearly, there is a need for further research to find out the true extent and type of bullying in secondary schools, to identify the main causes and ways in which bullying could best be prevented.

- Similarly, substantial minorities of students (especially in Year 9) indicated that they had played truant, albeit usually for a day or a lesson at a time. Further research, designed to go beyond the information to be published in league tables, which would map the extent and type of truancy in secondary schools, identify the main causes of truancy and provide examples of good practice in its prevention would clearly be of value to school managers, classroom teachers and educational administrators.

- The main purpose of this study was to provide information on students' motivation towards education and learning which would aid the National Commission on Education in the development of their recommendations. In order to meet the Commission's time scale, it was necessary to carry out a cross-sectional study comparing the responses of Year 7 and Year 9 students. A longitudinal study, following up the same cohort of students annually from Year 7 to the end of compulsory schooling (or even beyond), complemented by a more in-depth interview programme, would throw far more light on to the way students' motivation towards school and education develops throughout the secondary years by identifying the key stages and/ or events which affected students' attitudes. Such a study would clearly be of great value to all concerned with the education of young people.

APPENDIX 1

NATIONAL COMMISSION ON EDUCATION

The National Commission on Education was established in 1991 by the British Association for the Advancement of Science with the support of the Royal Society, the British Academy and the Fellowship of Engineering.

The Commission is a private venture, and has been made possible by a grant from the Paul Hamlyn Foundation. It is not associated in any way with any political party; the Prime Minister and leaders of the main opposition parties all welcomed its establishment.

The Commission's terms of reference are broad. They cover the whole of education and training and require the Commission to identify and examine the major developments likely to take place over the next 25 years. Working Groups have been established to investigate seven key issues, namely:

- Effective schooling
- Schools, society and citizenship
- The teaching profession and quality
- Higher and further education in the 21st century
- Preparing for work today and tomorrow
- Better ways of learning
- Resources.

The Commission's terms of reference range well beyond these designated topics and bring into play, especially over the longer term, many economic, social and other considerations which must be weighed in formulating recommendations for the development of education and training well into the next century.

Members of the Working Group on Schools, Society and Citizenship

Ms Margaret Maden, County Education Officer, Warwickshire (Chair)

Mrs Betty Campbell MBE, Head, Mount Stuart Primary School, Cardiff

Professor Bob Moon, School of Education, Open University

Mr Richard Holmes, Director, SE London Compact

Members of the National Commission on Education

Lord Walton of Detchant, House of Lords (Chairman)

Mr John Raisman CBE, Formerly Deputy Chairman, British Telecom (Deputy Chairman)

Sir John Cassels CB, Formerly Director, National Economic Development Office (Director)

Mrs Averil Burgess, Head, South Hampstead High School

Mrs Betty Campbell MBE, Head, Mount Stuart Primary School, Cardiff

Dr David Giachardi, Director of Research, Courtaulds plc

Mr Christopher Johnson, Formerly Economic Adviser, Lloyds Bank

Ms Helena Kennedy QC Barrister

Professor Alistair MacFarlane FRS FEng, Principal and Vice-Chancellor, Heriot Watt University

Ms Margaret Maden, County Education Officer, Warwickshire

Sir Claus Moser KCB CBE FBA, Warden, Wadham College, Oxford

Ms Jenny Shackleton, Principal, Wirral Metropolitan College

Mr Richard Staite, Head, Beeslack High School, Penicuik, Lothian

Professor Jeff Thompson CBE, Professor of Education, University of Bath

Professor David Watson, Director, Brighton Polytechnic

Mr Peter Wickens, Director of Personnel, Nissan Motor Manufacturing (UK) Ltd.

APPENDIX 2

THE DEVELOPMENT OF THE SCALES AND OTHER MEASURES FOR INCLUSION IN THE CORRELATION AND REGRESSION ANALYSES

A2.1 Introduction

The purpose of this Appendix is to describe the development of scales from the student questionnaire and to highlight the other items from the student and school questionnaires selected for inclusion in the correlation and regression analyses described in Appendix 3, which were intended to identify the factors associated with motivation towards school.

A2.2 The development of the scales from the student questionnaires

In selecting the scales for inclusion in the correlation and regression analyses, a balance had to achieved between the following considerations.

- The underlying factor structure: did the statements form a distinct group in factor analysis?

- The internal consistency of the scales: in terms of Cronbach's Alpha.

- The face validity of the scales: did the statements in each proposed scale appear to be describing the same dimension?

- The consistency of the scales between the Year 7 and Year 9 samples: was the underlying factor structure similar?

Initially, separate principal components analyses of the questionnaire responses of the Year 7 and Year 9 students were carried out and the varimax rotated factor structures examined for evidence of underlying factors. Each set of items was examined for internal consistency and scrutinised for face validity. In constructing the scales, items were reversed as appropriate so that a high score indicated a positive attitude and a low score meant a negative attitude. The five scales identified in this way are described below.

A2.2.1   The Positive Attitudes Towards School Scale

The Positive Attitudes Towards School Scale (Table A2.1) contained five positive and five negative items. It consisted of three items relating to liking for school and school work, three items focusing on interest or boredom with school work, three items which appeared to be concerned with the value of school work, and one item concerned with liking for teachers. The internal consistency of this scale was 0.84 for both age groups. This scale was chosen to be our criterion variable in the correlation and regression analyses described in Appendix 3

Table A2.1   The Positive Attitudes Towards School Scale

I am very happy when I am at school.
On the whole I like being at school.
Most of the time I don't want to go to school.

The work I do in lessons is interesting to me.
I am bored in lessons.
In a lesson I often count the minutes till it ends.

School work is worth doing.
The work I do in lessons is a waste of time.
School is a waste of time for me.

I like my teachers.

Internal consistency (Alpha): Year 7 = 0.84; Year 9 = 0.84

A2.2.2   The Positive School Ethos Scale

The Positive School Ethos Scale, which is shown in Table A2.2, consisted of nine items relating to the students' perceptions of some of the school and teaching factors shown by a number of previous studies to be systematically positively associated with students' attitudes towards school and education and with their behaviour in school (Part II, Section 4.4). The Positive School Ethos Scale included items concerned with the reputation of the school, the upkeep of the premises, clear rules of behaviour, firm discipline and good teaching practices (such as frequent praise, expecting high standards of work and regular marking). The internal consistency of the Positive School Ethos Scale was 0.71 for the Year 7 students and 0.75 for those in Year 9.

Table A2.2   The Positive School Ethos Scale

People think this is a good school.

My school is clean and tidy.

Most of my teachers always/usually/hardly ever mark my work.

My teachers make sure we do any homework that is set.

Most of my teachers try hard to make me work as well as I am able/are fairly easily satisfied/don't seem to care whether I work or not.

My teachers praise me when I do my work well.

The teachers in my school take action when they see anyone breaking school rules.

My teachers make it clear how we should behave in school.

My teachers can keep order in class.

Internal consistency (Alpha): Year 7 = 0.71; Year 9 = 0.75

A2.2.3 The Perceived Perseverance and Ability Scale

This scale, which measured students' perceptions of their ability at school work and how hard they worked, consisted of four items. Its internal consistency was 0.80 for the Year 7 students and 0.78 for those in Year 9. The scale is shown in Table A2.3.

Table A2.3   The Perceived Ability and Perseverance Scale

Student's perception of how good he/she is at school work.

Student's perception of how good teachers think he/she is at school work.

I get good marks for my work.

I work as hard as I can in school.

Internal consistency (Alpha): Year 7 = 0.80; Year 9 = 0.78

A2.2.4 The Utilitarian Purposes of School Scale

The Utilitarian Purposes of School Scale, shown in Table A2.4, consisted of six items, which appeared to fall into two separate subsets in terms of face validity. The first subset of items were related to what the students believed schools 'should' help students to do: pass examinations; get jobs; and become independent. The second set of items were concerned with the students' perceptions of the value their parents placed on school and schooling. It is not immediately clear why these two subsets of items load on the same factor, although it could be hypothesised that many young people unconsciously adopt their parents' values about school and schooling. The internal consistency of this scale was not very high: 0.58 for the Year 7 sample and 0.59 for the Year 9 sample.

Table A2.4   The Utilitarian Purposes of School Scale

Schools should help us to do as well as possible in exams like GCSE.
Schools should teach things that will be useful when we get jobs.
Schools should help us to be independent and stand on our own two feet.
School work doesn't help you get a job.
My parents think it is important for me to do well at school.
My parents think school is a waste of time.
My parents make it clear that I should behave well at school.

Internal consistency (Alpha): Year 7 = 0.58; Year 9 = 0.59

A2.2.5 The Talking Individually with Teachers Scale

This scale, which provided an indication of how frequently students talked individually with their teachers about their school work and career plans, contained four items. Its internal consistency was higher for the Year 9 sample (0.64) than for the Year 7 sample (0.41), presumably reflecting the greater involvement in careers decisions of the older students. The Talking Individually with Teachers Scale is shown in Table A2.5.

Table A2.5   The Talking Individually with Teachers Scale

How often have you talked to your class/form teacher about your school work?
How often have you talked to other teachers about your school work?
Do you talk to your class/form teacher about your career plans?
Do you talk to other teachers about your career plans?

Internal consistency (Alpha): Year 7 = 0.41; Year 9 = 0.64

A2.3   Other items from the students' questionnaire selected for inclusion in the regression analyses

A number of individual items from the student questionnaire were included in the regression analyses. These fell into two groups:

• Home background and parental support
• Student behaviour.

Where appropriate, items were reversed so that a high score indicated a positive response and a low score a negative response.

A2.3.1 Home background and parental support measures

The research described in Part II of this report is inconclusive with regard to the associations between socio-economic status and students' motivation towards education, although there is evidence from previous research linking parental support with positive attitudes and staying on at school (Part II, Section 4.2.2). A number of items focusing on home background and parental support were, therefore, included in the questionnaire.

- Number of books in the home.

- My parents are interested in how I do at school.

- My parents come to school parents evenings.

- After you have taken your exams at the end of Year 11, what do you think your parents want you to do?

- Do you talk to your parents about your career plans?

Although the items within the home background group appeared to be describing the same dimension, the factor analysis did not identify a coherent underlying factor structure. It was, therefore, decided to enter these measures in the regression analyses as separate items rather than as a single scale.

A2.3.2 Student behaviour

Previous research has shown that there is a link between students' attitudes towards school and their behaviour in school and it has been suggested that disaffection is the precursor of disruptive behaviour, truancy and early leaving (Part II, Section 2.2). The students taking part in the study were, therefore, asked several questions related to their behaviour in school. The following behaviour-related items were included in the regression analysis:

- How would you describe your behaviour in class and around school this year?

- How often have you had punishments, such as lines, detention or being kept in, this year?

- Have you ever played truant (bunked off/skived off) this year?

- How many hours each day do you normally spend doing homework?

As the factor analysis did not identify an underlying factor structure, these items were entered separately in the regression analyses.

The following item, which previous research has shown to be related to motivation towards school, but which did not form part of any of the factors identified, was also included in the regression analysis.

- After taking exams (e.g. GCSE), at the end of the fifth year (Year 11) ,what do you expect to do?

A copy of the student questionnaire is shown in Appendix 5.

A2.4   Items and scales from the school background questionnaire selected for inclusion in the regression analyses

Previous research is inconclusive about the relationship between school background factors and students' motivation towards school (Part II, Sections 2.2, 4.1.3 and 4.2.1). In order to throw further light on these relationships, a number of items concerned with school background factors were included in the correlation and regression analyses. These were.

Catchment Area 1: schools with mainly country town and/or rural catchment areas coded 1; otherwise 0.

Catchment Area 2: schools with mainly suburban catchment areas coded 1; otherwise 0.

Catchment Area 3: schools with mainly urban/inner-city catchment areas coded 1; otherwise 0.

District: schools in metropolitan LEAs coded 1; otherwise 0.

Type of school: independent or grammar schools coded 1; otherwise 0.

Free school meals: the approximate percentage of students receiving free school meals.

Ethnic minorities: the approximate percentage of students from ethnic minorities.

Reading age of intake: the approximate percentage of students in Year 7 with reading ages more than two years behind chronological ages at the beginning of Year 7.

GCSE results: the approximate percentage of students gaining five or more higher grade (A-C) GCSEs in 1990/91.

Monitoring and recording: this was a scale, derived from the school questionnaire, based on an arbitrary ranking of schools responses so that the Monitoring/recording processes used were arbitrarily ranked: Individual Action Plan (highest); Records of Achievement; Profiling/other; None (lowest); when a school used more than one process, it was scored for the highest ranked process.

Individual review: the proportion of students in the relevant age group given individual review/target setting sessions.

Time allocation for
individual review: Minimum annual time allocation per student in the relevant age group for one-to-one review.

A copy of the school background questionnaire is shown in Appendix 5.

APPENDIX 3

FACTORS ASSOCIATED WITH MOTIVATION TOWARDS SCHOOL AND LEARNING

In this appendix, the associations between students' motivation towards school and the range of school, student and home background variables described in Appendix 2 are examined and the relative strengths of these relationships are compared. The results of these analyses are described under the following main headings:

- The sub-scales within the Positive Attitudes Towards School Scale and their inter-correlations;

- The correlations between the Positive Attitudes Towards School Scale and the other scales and items included in the analyses;

- The results of the multilevel regression analyses.

The main implications from the results of these analyses are discussed in Chapters 5 and 6 of this report.

A3.1 The sub-scales within the Positive Attitudes Towards School Scale and their inter-correlations

The items forming the Positive Attitudes Towards School Scale appear on face value to fall into four distinct groups, even though they formed a single factor in the principle components analysis described in Appendix 2. The scale and its four component sub-scales are shown in Table A3.1 and the inter-correlations between the sub-scales are shown in Table A3.2.

i.   All the intercorrelations were moderate to strong, ranging from 0.39 - 0.58.

ii. Of particular interest were the correlations linking the Liking for School Sub-scale with:

- the Interest versus Boredom Subscale;

- the Liking for Teachers measure;

- the Value of School Sub-scale.

Liking for School Sub-scale:

   I am very happy when I am at school.
   On the whole, I like being at school.
   Most of the time I don't want to go to school.

Interest versus Boredom Sub-scale:

   The work I do in lessons is interesting to me.
   I am bored in lessons.
   In a lesson I often count the minutes till it ends.

Value of School Sub-scale:

   School work is worth doing.
   The work I do in lessons is a waste of time.
   School is a waste of time for me.

Liking for teachers:

   I like my teacher.

All items were re-scored so that a high score meant a positive attitude and a low score a negative attitude.

Table A.3.2 **Pearson Product Moment Correlations between Students' Liking for School, Interest/boredom in School, Perceptions of the Value of school and Liking for Teacher Sub-scales**

SUB-SCALES	1	2	3	4
1. Liking for School	..	58	55	53
2. Value of School	52	..	51	42
3. Interest/Boredom	48	53	..	41
4. Liking for Teachers	45	42	39	..

Decimal points omitted; all correlations are significant at the one per cent level; Year 7 correlation coefficients are above the diagonal and those for Year 9 below the diagonal.

A3.3 Correlations between the Positive Attitudes Towards School Scale and the other scales and items included in the analyses

Table A3.3 Pearson Product Moment Correlations between the Positive Attitudes Towards School Scale and the other items and scales included in the analyses

	Year 7	Year 9
Home measures		
Number of books in the home	09	08
My parents are interested in how I do at school.	24	25
My parents come to school parents evenings.	21	24
After Year 11, what do you think your parents want you to do?	17	21
Do you talk to your parents about your career plans?	17	26
School measures:		
School type	04	08
Metropolitan/non-metropolitan	03	00
Catchment Area 1: mainly rural	-01	-06
Catchment Area 2: mainly suburban	-03	-05
Catchment Area 3: mainly inner city	05	13
Free school meals (%)	01	07
Ethnic minorities (%)	07	10
Reading age of intake	-06	09
GCSE results (% gaining 5+ grades A-C)	09	03
School monitoring and recording procedures	06	08
Individual review	11	-05
Time allocated to individual review	04	-03
Student measures:		
The Positive School Ethos Scale	43	40
The Utilitarian Purposes of School Scale	39	38
The Talking Individually with Teachers Scale	08	21
Sex (1=boy, 0=girl)	-15	-14
The Perceived Ability and Perseverance Scale	41	40
How would you describe your behaviour?	29	38
How often have you had punishments this year?	23	36
Have you ever played truant this year?	-26	-24
How many hours each day do you spend doing homework?	24	29
After taking exams at the end of Year 11, what do you expect to do?	26	23

Decimal point omitted; correlation coefficients between 0.07 - 0.08 are significant at the five per cent level; correlation coefficients >0.08 are significant at the one per cent level; the numbers on which these correlation coefficients were based ranged from 820-1160 (Year 7) and 731-980 (Year 9).

The Positive Attitude Towards School Scale was selected as our outcome measure. This scale provides a composite measure of students' liking for school, their interest in school work, perceptions of the value of education and liking for their teachers. Students achieving a high score on this scale are likely to have positive attitudes towards school and learning and those obtaining a low score are likely to be hostile to school.

The purpose of the analyses described below is to identify some of the main factors associated with positive attitudes towards school and to compare the relative strengths of any associations found. Table A3.3 shows the simple correlations between our selected outcome variable, the Positive Attitudes Towards School Scale and the other items and scales included in the analyses (the predictor variables).

A3.3.1 The associations between the home measures included in the analyses and the Positive Attitudes Towards School Scale

i.   Our surrogate measure for the cultural level of the home (number of books in the home) was found to have very low associations (correlations of 0.09 and 0.08, respectively) with the Positive Attitudes Towards School Scale for both year groups.

ii.   However, the four measures concerned with students' perceptions of their parents' support   (interest in their child's progress and future career; attendance at school parents' evening; and high aspirations, in terms of wanting their child to remain in education) were found to be positively associated with the Positive Attitudes Towards School Scale (correlations ranging from 0.17 - 0.24, for Year 7 and from 0.21 - 0.26 for Year 9) .

A3.3.2 The associations between the school measures included in the analyses and the Positive Attitudes Towards School Scale

i.   An important finding of this study was the lack of association between the Positive Attitudes Towards School Scale and the school level intake and output measures used (type of school, type of catchment area, free school meals and reading age of intake and GCSE results) for either age group. Only 9 of the 30 correlations reported achieved statistical significance and only 2 were greater than 0.10. This appears to be consistent with the previous research reported in Part II (Section 4.2).

ii. However, some of the school measures included in the study were found to be linked with students' positive attitudes towards school and education. As Table A3.3 shows, there were significant positive associations between the Positive School Ethos Scale and the Positive Attitudes Towards School Scale (correlations of 0.43 and 0.40, respectively, for Year 7 and Year 9).

iii. The Utilitarian Purposes of School Scale, which gave a measure of students' views on the importance of the role of their schools in helping them to pass examinations, obtain employment and become independent, was found to have moderate associations (correlations of 0.39 and 0.38 for Year 7 and Year 9, respectively) with positive attitudes towards school and education.

A3.3.3 The associations between the student measures included in the analyses and the Positive Attitudes Towards School Scale

i. All the positively scored measures concerned with students' behaviour in school (the Perceived Ability and Perseverance Scale, behaviour in school, infrequent punishments and time spent of homework) were found to have moderate correlations (0.23 - 0.41) with the Positive Attitudes Toward School Scale, and the negatively scored item (which asked about truancy) was found to be significantly negatively associated.

ii. The item in our questionnaire concerned with staying on at school post-16 was found to be positively associated with our outcome measure .

iii. Finally, the negative association, shown in Table A3.3, between the variable 'sex' and the Positive Attitudes Towards School Scale confirmed that girls tend to have more positive attitudes towards school than do boys.

A3.4 The results of the multilevel regression analyses

Multilevel modelling was used to see which factors were important in explaining the Positive Attitudes Towards School Scale. The model has only two levels - school and student.

The initial models used student level variables such as sex, ethos scale, etc. and school level variables such as percentage of students from ethnic minorities or school level GCSE results (tables not shown). As a result of these initial analyses, many of the school level variables and some of the student level variables were dropped from the final analyses on the grounds that they were non-significant. This helped to increase the sample size available for modelling since not all the schools taking part in the study had provided background information.

A3.4.1 Year group and sex effects

A simple model was run to see whether positive attitudes towards school differed between boys and girls and between year groups, after allowing for home background, parental support and school background. The results of the analyses are shown in Table A3.4.

Table A3.4   Results from the multilevel regression - Year group and sex effects

Variables	Regression Coefficients
Constant	25.87 *
Number of books in home	0.00
My parents are interested in how I do at school.	1.14*
My parents come to school parents' evening.	0.58*
After Yr 11, what do you think your parents want you to do?	1.12*
Do you talk to your parents about your career plans?	0.92*
School type (Independent-grammar=1, Others=0)	-0.13
Area (Metropolitan=1, Non Metropolitan=0)	-0.08
School monitoring and recording procedures	0.51 *
Year group (1=Year 9, 0=Year7)	-1.09 *
Sex (1=boy, 0=girl)	-1.32 *

* Coefficient statistically significant at 5% level

i.   Table A3.4 shows that, after allowing for home background, parental support and school background, girls tended to have more positive attitudes than boys and that Year 7 students tended to have more positive attitudes than those in Year 9 .

ii. All the parental support items used in the regression were found to be significant, but the coefficient relating to the number of books in the home was not significant.

iii. The type or area of school did not have a significant effect but students in schools with monitoring procedures such as Individual Action Plan tended to have more positive attitudes than those in schools that did not have any such procedures.

A3.4.2   The full multilevel regression model

The next stage was to examine the effect of adding all the attitude scales and the student behaviour items into the analysis. The multilevel model was run separately for Year 7 and Year 9 students and with the two year groups combined. The results of the modelling are given in Table A3.5.

Table A3.5   Results from the multilevel regression - full model

Variables	Year 7	Year 9	Years 7&9
	<—— Coefficients ——>		
Constant	2.81	6.21*	4.30*
Number of books in home.	-0.03	-0.21	-0.10
My parents are interested in how I do at school.	0.41	0.15	0.31*
My parents come to school parents' evening.	-0.08	0.16	0.04
After Yr 11, what do you think your parents want you to do?	0.15	0.34	0.22
Do you talk to your parents about your career plans?	0.08	0.50*	0.22
School type (Independent-grammar=1, Others=0)	-0.06	-0.44	-0.41
Area (Metropolitan=1, Non Metropolitan=0)	-0.63	0.06	-0.20
School monitoring and recording procedures	0.31	0.42	0.38*
Year group (1=Year 9, 0=Year7)	n/a	n/a	-0.10
The Positive School Ethos scale	0.31*	0.19*	0.25*
The Utilitarian Purposes of School Scale	0.39*	0.31*	0.36*
The Perceived ability and perserverence Scale	0.33*	0.38*	0.37*
The Talking Individually with Teachers Scale	-0.01	0.12	0.05
How often have you had punishments this year? (scale reversed)	0.47*	0.99*	0.70*
Have you ever played truant this year?	-2.32*	-0.89*	-1.45*
How many hours each day do you spend doing homework?	0.37*	0.22*	0.29*
After taking exams at the end of Yr 11, what do you expect to do?	1.18*	0.81*	1.04*
Sex (1=Boy, 0=Girl)	-1.05*	-0.48	-0.80*

* Coefficient statistically significant at 5% level

i. The Positive School Ethos Scale, the Utilitarian Purposes of School Scale and the Perceived Ability and Perseverance Scales were found to be significant factors, but the Talking Individually with Teachers Scale did not appear to be a significant factor in explaining students' attitudes towards school.

ii. Whereas all the parental support items and the year group were significant in the previous model (see Table A3.4), most of these were not significant in the new model shown in Table A3.5. This does not mean that these variables were no longer important, but reflects the fact that they were to some extent correlated with the new variables added to the model.

iii. The three behaviour items used were all significant: receiving less punishment during the year and doing more homework were associated with having a more positive attitude towards school; and playing truant with a more negative attitude. Students who had decided to carry on with their education after the end of the fifth year tended to have more positive attitudes towards school.

iv. The results were reasonably consistent between Year 7 and Year 9 and when the two year groups were combined. However, there were a few differences: for example the item concerned with talking to parents about career plans was a significant factor at Year 9 but not at Year 7, although this is probably not unexpected as few students are likely to be seriously considering their careers at Year 7.

A3.4.3 *The variation in the Positive Attitudes Towards Schools Scale*

Table A3.6 Variation in the Postive Attitudes Toward School Scale

Variables	Year 7	Year 9	Years 7&9
Total variance	24.97	21.41	23.62
Between schools (%)	8%	9%	9%
Between students within schools (%)	92%	91%	91%

Percentage of between student variance accounted for by the model

Variables	Year 7	Year 9	Years 7&9
Number of books in home	1%	0%	1%
My parents are interested in how I do at school. My parents come to school parents' evening. After Yr 11, what do you think your parents want you to do? Do you talk to your parents about your career plans?	10%	13%	11%
The Positive School Ethos Scale	12%	8%	10%
The Utilitarian Purposes of School Scale	4%	3%	3%
The Perceived ability and Perserverence Scale	5%	6%	6%
The Talking Individually with Teachers Scale	0%	0%	0%
How often have you had punishments this year? Have you ever played truant this year? How many hours each day do you spend doing homework?	4%	4%	4%
After taking exams at the end of Yr 11, what do you expect to do?	1%	1%	1%
Sex (1=boy, 0=girl)	1%	0%	1%
Total between pupil variation explained	38%	36%	36%

i. Table A3.6 shows the amount of variation in the Positive Attitude Towards School Scale between schools and pupils. Most of the variation in the scale was due to differences between pupils within schools and less than ten per cent of the total variation was due to differences between schools. It seems likely that this low percentage of between school variation contributed to the lack of association between the attitude scale and school level intake measures not only in this study but also in previous research.

ii. Around 36 percent of the variation between students was explained by the variables in the model. The items in the regression model were added in the order shown in Table A3.6 with some of the items entered in blocks: the home and parental items were entered first on the grounds that they pre-existed the school in the life of the student; the school-related variables entered next; and the student measures entered last on the grounds that students are likely to be influenced by both home/parental and school factors .

iii. The cumulative effects of adding variables can be seen here. When entered first in the analyses, the home and parental measures explain around 11 - 13 per cent of the between pupil variance. The Positive School Ethos Scale explained a further 8 - 12 per cent of the variance; and the Utilitarian Purposes-Scale a further three to four per cent; the Perceived Ability and Perseverance Scale accounted for a further six per cent; and the student's sex and intention to stay on each accounted for a further one per cent.

iv. To summarise, the parental support measures explained about 11 - 13 per cent of the variance in students' attitudes towards school, the Positive School Ethos Scale and the Utilitarian Purposes Scale together explained 11 - 16 per cent; and student measures (perceived ability, behaviour, sex and intention to stay on) together explained about 11 - 12 per cent .

APPENDIX 4
ADMINISTRATION AND RESPONSE RATES

It was intended to achieve two samples, each consisting of about 1,000 students in about 50 schools, in Year 7 and Year 9 respectively. The samples of schools were drawn from the Register of Schools, an annually upated database of all schools in England and Wales maintained by the NFER. Previous experience suggested that the response rate from secondary schools during the latter part of the summer term would be about 70 per cent. The initial samples drawn from the Register of Schools each, therefore, consisted of 75 schools.

These schools were invited to take part in the study and asked to provide us with a list of the relevant tutor groups: 51 schools drawn in the Year 7 sample and 46 drawn in the Year 9 sample agreed to participate. One tutor group was then randomly selected by NFER (using random number tables) from each participating school and questionnaires for that tutor group dispatched to the school. The headteacher of each school was also asked to arrange for the completion of a short school questionnaire.

Timetable

Schools invited to participate	20 May 1992
First reminder	3 June 1992
Questionnaires dispatched to schools	15 June 1992
First reminder	10 July 1992
Second reminder (telephone)	21 July 1992

Due to the short timescale of the project, one postal reminder only was sent at each stage.

Table A4.1   Response from schools

	2715 Year 7	2716 Year 9
Schools drawn in sample	75	75
Withdrawn by LEA	2	3
Request not to be included	1	1
No pupils in age range	1	
Total withdrawn	4	4
Schools contacted initially	71	7
Refused	11	18
No reply	9	7
Agreed to take part and sent questionnaires	51	46
Returned questionnaires	47	43
Response rate from of schools contacted initially	66%	61%
Response rate from schools agreeing to take part and sent questionnaires	92%	93%

The reasons given by schools for refusal to take part are given below:

- Involved with National Curriculum Assessment   7
- Too many requests for surveys   7
- Staff under too much pressure   8
- School reorganising/closing   3
- Fire in school   1
- Survey too difficult to administer   1
- No benefit to school   1
- No reason given   1

Table A4.2   Numbers of questionnaires dispatched and returned

Student questionnaire	Year 7	Year 9
Questionnaires dispatched	1362	1194
Questionnaires returned uncompleted (i.e. from schools returning at least one questionnaire)	118	131
Questionnaires not returned (i.e. schools failing to return any questionnaires)	84	83
Completed questionnaires received	1160	980

School questionnaire	Year 7	Year 9
School questionnaires dispatched to schools	51	46
School questionnaires received back	44	39
Not returned from schools returning student questionnaires	3	4
Not returned from schools not returning anything	4	3

The seven schools which failed to return any questionnaires were all telephoned before the end of term, but no parcels were received from them.

APPENDIX 5

THE QUESTIONNAIRES

The School background questionnaire and the student questionnaire for Year 9 students are presented in this Appendix. The questionnaire for Year 7 students is not included as it was substantially the same as the questionnaire for Year 9 students.

School No.

STUDENTS' ATTITUDES TO EDUCATION

SCHOOL BACKGROUND QUESTIONNAIRE

A study being carried out on behalf of the
National Commission on Education

Please return the completed questionnaire, together with the
student questionnaires (A), to the NFER, using the pre-paid label
provided, within two weeks of receipt.

If you have any queries please contact:
Field Research Services, NFER, The Mere,
Upton Park, Slough, Berkshire. SL1 2DQ (0753) 574123 Ext. 272.

CONFIDENTIAL

National Foundation for Educational Research in England and Wales

2715/6   **B**

I: BACKGROUND INFORMATION ON THE SCHOOL

It would be helpful if you could provide the following background information on your school. If you cannot provide exact numbers or percentages, please make the best estimates you can.

1.1 Please indicate the age range of school   (please circle)

Age range

5 - 12/13 years... 1

7/8 - 12/13 years 2

10/11 - 14 years 3

10/11/12/13 - 16 years... 4   10

11/12/13 - 18/19 years... 5

Other (please specify and circle)................................. 6

....

1.2 For **all** schools: (please enter number)

Approximate number of students on the roll
(as at January 1992)   11-14

(please enter percentages
to **nearest whole number**)

Approximate percentage of students:

from ethnic minority groups.. %   15-17

receiving free school meals.. %   18-20

1.3 Type of catchment area: (please circle)

mainly country town and/or rural 1

mainly suburban 2   21

mainly urban/inner city 3

1.4 For all schools with **Year 7** students (11-12 year olds) on the roll: (please enter number)

No. of students in Year 7 in 1991/92................................   22-4

(please enter percentage
to **nearest whole number**)

Approximate percentage of students in Y7 with
reading ages more than 2 years behind chronological .... %   25-7
ages at the beginning of Year 7.

QUESTIONS 1.5 AND 1.6 RELATE TO THE SCHOOL YEAR 1990/91 (LAST YEAR)

1.5   For all schools with **Year 11** students (15-16 year olds) on the roll in 1990/91

(please enter numbers)

No. of students in Year 11 in **1990/91 (last school year)** .... [   ]   28-30

Approximate number of these students gaining five or more
higher grade (A-C) GCSEs.. [   ]   31-33

Approximate number of these students who continued
their full-time education (ie either went into the sixth form in your
school or another school or to a sixth form college or college of FE) .... [   ]   34-36

1.6   For all schools with **Year 13** students (17-18 year olds)
(second year sixth) on the roll in 1990/91

(please enter numbers)

No. of students in Year 13 in **1990/91 (last school year)** .... [   ]   37-39

Approximate number who obtained 2 or more A-levels
grades A-E or equivalent (ie. AS levels, BTEC National
Diploma) in Summer 1991 .... [   ]   40-42

Approximate number going on to some form of higher
education (eg. degree, HND) .... [   ]   43-45

II: SUPPORTING KEY STAGE 3 STUDENTS

2.1   Since September 1991, how has the overall progress of individual students been formally
monitored/recorded in your school?

(Please circle all the ticks that apply for each year group)

	Year 7	Year 8	Year 9	
Through an emphasis on the profiling process	✓	✓	✓	46,7,8
Through the use of a Record of Achievement	✓	✓	✓	49,50,5
Through the use of an Individual Action Plan	✓	✓	✓	52.3.4
Other (please circle and specify on appropriate lines below)	✓	✓	✓	55,6,7

Y7 ....

Y8 ....

Y9 ....

2.2 **Since September 1991,** have individual (one-to-one) review/target-setting sessions been provided/planned for Key Stage 3 students?

(Please circle as appropriate)

	Year 7 students			Year 8 students			Year 9 students			
	All	Some	None	All	Some	None	All	Some	None	
With the form/group tutor?	1	2	3	1	2	3	1	2	3	58,9,60
With other teachers?	1	2	3	1	2	3	1	2	3	61,2,3

2.3 What is the minimum <u>annual</u> time allocation per student for one-to-one review in 1991/2?

(Please circle one number in each column)

	Year 7	Year 8	Year 9	
Less than 30 minutes	1	1	1	
30-60 minutes	2	2	2	64,5,6
Over 60 minutes	3	3	3	

2.4 How does the school consult with Year 9 pupils and their parents about GCSE options for Years 10/11?

(Please circle a tick for all that apply)

General meeting(s) for parents	✓	67
Talks/discussions with group/classes of students	✓	68
Talks/discussions with whole of Year 9 together	✓	69
Option scheme (eg options booklet) sent to parents	✓	70
Individual interviews with **all** students	✓	71
Individual interviews with **some** students	✓	72
Individual interviews with **all** parents	✓	73
Individual interviews with **some** parents	✓	74
Other (please specify and circle)	✓	75

....

THANK YOU VERY MUCH FOR COMPLETING THIS QUESTIONNAIRE

Please return the completed questionnaire to the NFER, together with the student questionnaires (A), using the jiffy bag in which they were sent and the pre-paid label provided.

I-95

YOU AND YOUR SCHOOL
A questionnaire for
Year 9 students

A study being carried out on behalf of the
National Commission on Education

This is not a test. The questions have been designed so that you can let us know how you feel about your school and schoolwork.

All your answers will be treated as CONFIDENTIAL

National Foundation for Educational Research in England and Wales

2716 **A**

SECTION 1: YOU AND YOUR SCHOOL

1.1   Look at the sentences below.

We want you to read each one and then see whether you agree or not with what has been said.
When you have decided, circle the number in the column that is closest to what you feel.

Example:

	Strongly agree	*Agree*	*Disagree*	*Strongly disagree*	*Not sure*
(a) *I like watching television*	①	2	3	4	5
(b) *I like rainy days*	1	2	③	4	5

*In (a) I have circled the number 1 in the **strongly agree** column to show that I agree with this
sentence because I like watching television very much.*

*In (b) I have circled the number 3 in the **disagree** column to show that I disagree with this
sentence because I do not like rainy days.*

	Strongly agree	Agree	Disagree	Strongly disagree	Not sure	
						Card 1
I am very happy when I am at school	1	2	3	4	5	10
My school has sensible rules	1	2	3	4	5	11
Homework is important in helping me to do well at school	1	2	3	4	5	12
Schools should teach things that will be useful when we get jobs	1	2	3	4	5	13
Schools should help us to do as well as possible in exams like GCSE	1	2	3	4	5	14

continued on next page

	Strongly agree	Agree	Disagree	Strongly disagree	Not sure	NFER use
School is a waste of time for me	1	2	3	4	5	15
School work is worth doing	1	2	3	4	5	16
Schools should help us to be independent and stand on our own two feet	1	2	3	4	5	17
Most of the time I don't want to go to school	1	2	3	4	5	18
My parents think it is important for me to do well at school	1	2	3	4	5	19
My parents think school is a waste of time	1	2	3	4	5	20
People think this is a good school	1	2	3	4	5	21
Schools should help us to learn how to use our spare (leisure) time	1	2	3	4	5	22
My parents make it clear that I should behave well in school	1	2	3	4	5	23
School work doesn't help you get a job	1	2	3	4	5	24
On the whole I like being at school	1	2	3	4	5	25
I like lessons where I can work with my friends	1	2	3	4	5	26
I like lessons where I can work on my own	1	2	3	4	5	27
I like lessons where I can make something	1	2	3	4	5	28
I like lessons where we have discussions	1	2	3	4	5	29

continued on next page

1.2   Please answer the questions below by circling the number which is closest to what you think
        is true.

Example:

	All lessons	*Most lessons*	*Some lessons*	*Hardly any lessons*	*No lessons*
I use a pen or pencil	*1*	*②*	*3*	*4*	*5*

*I have circled the number 2 to show that I use a pen or pencil in **most lessons***

	All lessons	Most lessons	Some lessons	Hardly any lessons	No lessons	
I work as hard as I can in school	1	2	3	4	5	30
In a lesson, I often count the minutes till it ends	1	2	3	4	5	31
I am bored in lessons	1	2	3	4	5	32
The work I do in lessons is a waste of time	1	2	3	4	5	33
The work I do in lessons is interesting to me	1	2	3	4	5	34
I get good marks for my work	1	2	3	4	5	35
I am keen to answer questions in class	1	2	3	4	5	36

1.3   Please answer the questions below by circling the number which is closest to what you think
        is true.

	Always	Nearly always	Sometimes	Hardly ever	Never	
My parents are interested in how I do at school	1	2	3	4	5	37
My parents come to school parents' evenings	1	2	3	4	5	38
My parents make sure I do my homework	1	2	3	4	5	39
My school is clean and tidy	1	2	3	4	5	40

continued on next page

1.4   Please answer the questions below by circling the number which is closest to what you think is
true.

	All teachers	Most teachers	Some teachers	Hardly any teachers	No teachers	
My teachers make sure we do any homework that is set	1	2	3	4	5	41
My teachers make it clear how we should behave in school	1	2	3	4	5	42
The teachers in my school take action when they see anyone breaking school rules	1	2	3	4	5	43
My teachers praise me when I do my school work well	1	2	3	4	5	44
I like my teachers	1	2	3	4	5	45
My teachers can keep order in class	1	2	3	4	5	46

**MOST OF THE REST OF THE QUESTIONS SHOULD BE ANSWERED BY CIRCLING
ONE NUMBER**

Example:

The weather today is:

too hot.................................. 1
about right........................... 2
too cold................................ ③

I have circled the number 3, because I think the weather today is too cold

SECTION 2:   SCHOOL RULES AND DISCIPLINE

2.1   Do you think the discipline in your school is:

too strict?.. 1

about right?.. 2   47

not strict enough?... 3

continued on next page

2.2   Does your school have:

too many rules?...1

about the right number of rules?.......................................2

not enough rules?..3

2.3   How would you describe your behaviour in class and around school this year (Year 9) and in previous years (Year 8 and Year 7)?

(please circle one number for each year)

	Year 9 (this year)	Year 8 (last year)	Year 7
Always well behaved....................	1	1	1
Usually well behaved...................	2	2	2
Sometimes badly behaved	3	3	3
Often badly behaved.....................	4	4	4

2.4a) Have you ever played truant (bunked off/skived off) this year or in previous years?

(please circle one number for each year)

	Year 9 (this year)	Year 8	Year 7
Yes	1	1	1
No	2	2	2

b)   If **yes**, how often?

(please circle one number for each year)

	Year 9 (this year)	Year 8	Year 7
A lesson here and there	1	1	1
A day here and there....................	2	2	2
Several days at a time...................	3	3	3
Weeks at a time..............................	4	4	4
Does not apply................................	5	5	5

continued on next page

2.5 How often have you had punishments, such as lines, detention, being kept in etc. this year and in previous years?

(please circle one number for each year)

	Year 9 (this year)	Year 8	Year 7
Never	1	1	1
Once or twice.................................	2	2	2
Quite often	3	3	3
Often	4	4	4

2.6 Have you ever been bullied or badly treated by other students in school?

(please circle one number for each year)

	Year 9 (this year)	Year 8	Year 7
Never	1	1	1
Once or twice	2	2	2
Quite often	3	3	3
Often	4	4	4

2.7 Do you like school:

more than you did last year?... 1

about the same as you did last year?... 2

less than you did last year?.. 3

SECTION 3: YOUR TEACHERS

3.1 Most of my teachers:

try hard to make me work as well as I am able.......................... 1

are fairly easily satisfied... 2

don't seem to care whether I work or not................................. 3

continued on next page

3.2   Most of my teachers:

        always mark my work 1

        usually mark my work... 2   66

        hardly ever mark my work...................................... 3

3.3   Since September 1991, have you talked **on your own** to a teacher about your school work?

	With your class/ form teacher	With any other teacher
Often.................................	1	1
Sometimes.........................	2	2
Never	3	3

67,68

SECTION 4:   ACTIVITIES OUTSIDE LESSON TIME

4.1a) Does your school have any lunch-hour or after school activities run by your teachers?

        Yes 1

        No 2   69

b)   If **yes**, do you take part in any of these activities?

        Yes... 1

        No.. 2   70

4.2   How many **HOURS EACH DAY** do you normally spend doing homework?

        I am not usually given homework........................ 1

        I am given homework but I don't do it................ 2

        Half an hour or less... 3   71

        About 1 hour.. 4

        About 1 and a half hours... 5

        About 2 hours.. 6

        About 2 and half hours... 7

        3 hours or more... 8

continued on next page

4.3   How many **HOURS EACH DAY** do you watch television/videos?

0-1 hours.. 1

about 2 hours.. 2

about 3 hours.. 3

about 4 hours.. 4

about 5 hours.. 5

6 hours or more.. 6

4.4   How often do you read on your own for fun outside school?

every day/almost every day... 1

once or twice a week... 2

once or twice a month 3

never or hardly ever 4

SECTION 5:   YOU AND YOUR FUTURE

5.1a) After taking exams (eg. GCSE) at the end of the fifth year (Year 11) do you expect to:

go into the sixth form of this school... 1

go to another school or college 2

get a job as soon as possible... 3

not sure 4

b)   If you circled 1 or 2 (ie you expect to stay on at school or go to college) what do
       you intend to do **after that**?

Go on to university, polytechnic or other college 1

Get a job as soon as possible.. 2

Not sure 3

5.2   What do you think that your parents want you to do?

Go on to university, polytechnic or other college 1

Get a job as soon as possible 2

Not sure 3

continued on next page

5.3a) Have you decided what job or career you would like to have?

Yes 1

No 2

b)   If **yes,** please write the name of the job or career in the box below

```



```

c)   If **yes**, will you need any qualifications (eg GCSE, A-levels) to get the job you want?

Yes 1

No 2

Not sure 3

5.4   Do you talk to any of the following people about your career plans?

	Often	Sometimes	Never/ Hardly ever	
Your parents	1	2	3	14
Brothers or sisters	1	2	3	15
Other family members	1	2	3	16
Your friends	1	2	3	17
Your form tutor	1	2	3	18
Any other teachers	1	2	3	19
Any other person	1	2	3	20

SECTION 6:   YOU AND YOUR FAMILY

6.1   Are you:

Male 1

Female 2

continued on next page

I-105

6.2 How many brothers and/or sisters do you have? (Don't count yourself)

One.. 1

Two.. 2

Three.. 3

Four... 4

Five or more.. 5

6.3 How good do you think you are at school work?

Very good.. 1

Above average.. 2

Average... 3

Below average... 4

Not at all good.. 5

6.4 How do you think your teachers would describe your school work?

Very good.. 1

Above average.. 2

Average... 3

Below average... 4

Not at all good..5

6.5 **APPROXIMATELY**, how many books are there in your home?
(Do not count newspapers, magazines or comics)

0-10... 1

11-25... 2

26-100 (about one bookcase full).............. 3

101-250 (about two bookcases full).......... 4

251-500 (about three bookcases full)....... 5

More than 500... 6

continued on next page

NFER use

6.6a) Does either of your parents read a daily newspaper most days?

Yes.. 1

No.. 2

Don't know.. 3

26

b) If YES, please tick the name of the newspaper(s).

Sun .... ☐	Daily Telegraph .... ☐		27, 28
Daily Mirror .... ☐	Guardian .... ☐		29, 30
Daily Star................ ☐	Times.. ☐		31, 32
Daily Mail .... ☐	Independent.................................... ☐		33, 34
Daily Express........... ☐	Financial Times.............................. ☐		35, 36
Today...................... ☐	Other (please give name of paper).* ☐		37, 38

*...

39-40

SECTION 7: YOUR COMMENTS

7.1 Thinking about **your** future, what are the most important ways your school could help you?

41-2

43-4

45-6

7.2 Is there anything else, good or bad, you would like to write about your school?

47-8

49-50

51-52

THANK YOU VERY MUCH FOR COMPLETING THIS QUESTIONNAIRE

Please seal the completed questionnaire in the envelope provided and return it to your teacher

PART II

A REVIEW OF THE RESEARCH LITERATURE ON MOTIVATION TOWARDS SCHOOL AND LEARNING

CHAPTER 1
INTRODUCTION

The main purpose of this review was to provide insights into the findings of previous research into students' motivation towards school and education, in order to help the Commission's Working Group on Schools, Society and Citizenship develop and refine its recommendations on the future of education in Great Britain. A secondary purpose was to complement and add greater weight to the findings of our research into factors associated with motivation towards school and learning which are described in Part I of this report.

After a brief examination of the nature of motivation, this review examines the research into factors associated with positive and negative attitudes towards school and education. Research into the factors associated with behavioural indicators of disaffection (disruptive behaviour in school, truancy and early leaving) has also been included, where relevant, but research into factors associated with pupils' attitudes to different school subjects has not been examined in detail. Finally, a number of accounts of the ways in which practitioners (in the United Kingdom, the United States and Europe) have attempted to improve students' achievement, attitudes, attendance rates, behaviour and dropout rates have been examined.

This review is not intended to be an exhaustive survey of the literature on motivation towards school and education. Many previous studies have already examined aspects of this literature quite thoroughly. For example, Rutter *et al.* (1979), Rutter (1983), Mortimore *et al.* (1988), Purkey and Smith (1983) and Weindling (1989) have already provided detailed analyses of the literature on school improvement, much of which is pertinent to this review. Their main findings with regard to the relationship between school factors and students' attitudes are summarised in Section 4.4 of this review.

CHAPTER 2
WHAT IS MOTIVATION TOWARDS SCHOOL AND LEARNING?

2.1 Motivation to learn

According to Entwistle (1988), psychologists have described motivation in terms of drive, or the amount of energy directed to some goal or towards the satisfaction of some need. In the past, it was considered to be a more or less fixed characteristic of the individual. However, Entwistle (op. cit.) argues that there are various forms of academic motivation which derive from different sources of reward and punishment.

Firstly, he distinguishes between intrinsic and extrinsic motivation: intrinsic motivation arises from attitudes to the subject matter itself, whereas extrinsic motivation depends upon external rewards. Intrinsic motivation, according to Entwistle, tends to be linked with a deep approach to learning (the desire to reach understanding of a subject or topic), whereas extrinsic motivation tends to be linked with a surface approach to learning (for example, the desire to get good marks).

Secondly, he makes the distinction between 'need for achievement' and 'fear of failure': need for achievement is the search for success with a view to boosting self-esteem, whereas fear of failure anticipates a threat to self-esteem.

Thirdly, he argues that students can attribute their success or failure either to internal factors (ability, effort, strategies) or to external factors (bad luck, difficulty, unfairness). A student who explains his failure by an internal reason, such as lack of effort, may react to failure by trying harder: he may succeed, thus boosting his self-esteem; or he may 'fail', resulting in lowered self-esteem and disaffection. Similarly, a student who attributes his failure to external reasons can easily become disaffected since he is likely to feel powerless to improve his performance.

Entwistle (1988) points out that students who fear failure may 'put effort into avoiding effort'. They appear to be trying to avoid situations where they expect to fail (Rollett, 1987). Veerman (1987) argues that 'these so-called non-motivated children and adolescents' would like to succeed at school, but have simply given up hope. Such students easily become disaffected or disengaged from school and learning.

2.2 The outcomes of disaffection

It has been argued that disruptive behaviour, truancy, early leaving and dropout are all outcomes of disaffection.

Several research studies have suggested that disruptive behaviour and truancy are the 'crystallisation of disaffection from school' (Ouston and Maughan, 1985; Robinson, 1990), rather than an activity undertaken solely because of conditions at home or in the family and, further, that dropping out can be viewed as 'a dynamic process of slow, cumulative disengagement from school' (Rumberger, 1987; Wehlage and Rutter, 1986). Truancy (and disruptive behaviour), however, have an adverse effect, not only on the truant, but also on other students and on the atmosphere of the school (Elton, 1989).

Studies in England (Morton-Williams and Finch, 1968; Kysel *et al.*, 1992) and in the United States (Ekstrom *et al.*, 1986; Wehlage and Rutter, 1986) have identified a number of student- and home-related factors which tend to be associated with early leaving or dropout:

- disillusionment with and dislike of school;

- a belief that school would not improve their career prospects;

- low educational aspirations;

- lack of interest and effort in class and less time spent on homework;

- disruptive behaviour and resentment of rules;

- poor academic achievement;

- poor attendance and truancy;

- lack of parental interest and support;

- low socio-economic status.

The research on factors associated with motivation towards school and learning, which is discussed in detail in Section 4 of this review, shows that many of the above factors are also associated with disaffection and negatively associated with favourable attitudes towards school and learning.

CHAPTER 3

THE MEASUREMENT OF MOTIVATION TOWARDS SCHOOL AND LEARNING

Pupils attitudes towards school and learning have often been measured by means of attitude inventories (for example Entwistle and Kozeki,1985; Gray, McPherson and Raffe, 1983; MacBeath and Weir, 1991; Brighouse,1992; Ainley and Bourke, 1992; Williams and Batten, 1981). These usually consist of a series of statements to which the student has to respond on a two-, three-, four- or five-point scale by circling a number or ticking a box.

Example

	Strongly agree	Agree	Disagree	Strongly disagree	Not sure
I like school.	1	2	3	4	5
School is a waste of time.	1	2	3	4	5

Normally, an inventory will include several attitudinal scales and contain up to ten items (positive and negative) purporting to measure each scale (for example a liking for school scale). A student's score on a scale is calculated by simple or weighted addition of his/her scores on the items making up the scale (after suitably reversing the scores of negative items).

Typically, attitude inventories have included scales purporting to measure students' attitudes to school, school work, teachers, teaching approaches and school subjects (see, for example, Ormerod and Duckworth's (1975) review of research on attitudes to science.)

Other researchers have used a more qualitative approach, some by interviewing disaffected students (for example Bealing, 1990; Robinson, 1990; Weston, 1990) to try to identify the underlying reasons for disaffection, and others by interviewing students to find out their views of school (for example Blatchford, 1992).

FACTORS ASSOCIATED WITH MOTIVATION TOWARDS SCHOOL AND LEARNING

4.1 Societal factors and motivation

4.1.1 Job and career prospects

There is ample research evidence that many students and their parents believe that an important purpose of school and education is to help them get a job or set them on the path for their chosen career. Kysel *et al.* (1992), Dean (1982a, 1982b), Varlaam and Shaw (1984) all found that the main reasons given by students for staying on at school were concerned with gaining qualifications which would improve their employment prospects, and the early leavers and their parents taking part in Morton-Williams and Finch's (1968) study believed that the main objective of secondary education should be 'to provide the knowledge and skills to enable young people to obtain the best jobs and careers of which they were capable'. There is evidence, too, that this belief is held by quite young children. Blatchford (1992), in an interview study of 175 11-year-olds in inner London primary schools, found that the most frequent reason given for doing well at school was help with future employment and career once they had left school.

It could be argued that disaffected students may be more likely to respond positively to a school curriculum which is clearly linked to the world of work. However, as Entwistle (1988) points out, 'without a substantial change in the employment situation teachers may well be fighting a losing battle to maintain interest and morale among their pupils'. On the other hand, the work of Raffe (1986) 'challenges arguments alleging the demotivation and demoralising effect of unemployment' on school students. He found that rates of truancy amongst fourth-year students in Scotland declined over a period when national unemployment figures were rising sharply and that truancy rates were lower in areas of high unemployment.

4.1.2 Peer group pressures

It has been suggested that the peer group plays an important part in the development of individuals during adolescence and that it affects attitudes, beliefs and behaviour (Douglas, 1983; Schmuck, 1977). In order to be accepted by his friends, an adolescent tries to comply with the norms and rules of his chosen friendship group. This was partly illustrated by a small-scale sociometric study of one class of 14 to 15-year-olds, carried out by Winiarski-Jones (1988), which demonstrated that the mean academic performance of students who were members of the 'anti-authority' clique was lower than that of members of the 'academic' clique. However, she found no differences in academic motivation between the two groups, which led her to hypothesise that clique membership may affect a student's behaviour but not necessarily change internalised attitudes and beliefs.

4.1.3   Inner cities

'Urban education is regarded as a major problem in many of the developed countries of the world. Policies designed to cope with underachievement have often been "fragmented, temporary and reactive rather than pre-emptive and preventative"'(Mortimore, 1991). However, although researchers have observed that students are likely to achieve less well in urban than in other sorts of schools, they have also emphasised that some of these schools are very effective in promoting students' progress. The evidence from the school effectiveness studies (reported in Section 4.4) and the Educational Priority Area Project carried out in the early 1970s (reported in Section 5.1) suggests that urban schools could have a major part to play in the regeneration of urban society' (Mortimore, op. cit.).

However, the Annual Reports of HM Senior Chief Inspector of Schools for 1988/89, 1989/90 and 1990/91 express concern about the extent of truancy in schools in inner city and/or disadvantaged areas. In his report for 1990/91, the Senior Chief Inspector states: 'In inner city areas the average attendance was less than 80 per cent for the school as a whole and dropped below 50 per cent for Year 11.'

In addition. several studies (for example, GB. DES, 1982; Gray and Jesson, 1987) have shown that achievement in terms of public examination results and staying on rates both tend to be lower in inner cities than elsewhere.

4.2 Parent and home factors and motivation

4.2.1 Socio-economic status

There has been very little research into the relationship between family background and pupils' attitudes towards school and education amongst secondary school students. However, research examining this relationship amongst top primary students (Ainley and Bourke, 1992) and research into factors affecting students' attitudes towards science (Keys, 1987) suggests that the associations are either weak or non-existent. Further confirmation comes from recent research carried out in Glasgow by Croxford and McPherson (in press), who found that school leavers with lower socio-economic status backgrounds held slightly more positive attitudes towards school and teachers than those with higher socio-economic status backgrounds. Both groups, however, held quite positive attitudes towards school and teachers.

On the other hand, in a study carried out in Sheffield (Galloway *et al.*, 1985) poor school attendance - arguably an outcome of disaffection - was found to be strongly associated with socio-economic disadvantage: two housing variables (living in furnished tenancies and shared dwellings) were found to be significant predictors of absenteeism. It may well be that, whereas students' attitudes are relatively unrelated to socio-economic factors, their behaviour is more likely to be adversely affected by socio-economic disadvantage.

Students' achievement, also, has been found to be quite strongly associated with socio-economic status (Coleman *et al.*, 1966; Jencks *et al.*, 1972; Plowden, 1967; Gray McPherson and Raffe, 1983; Ekstrom *et al.*, 1986; Rumberger, 1983; Keys, 1987; Kysel *et al.*, 1992). The majority of these studies found that family background could explain between 25 and 70 per cent of the variation in pupils' achievement. Few studies have been able to explain the process, although research has also shown that certain family-related factors, often believed to characterise high socio-economic status parents, are positively related to attainment. These are: parental involvement in child's education (Fehrmann *et al.*, 1987; Wedge and Prosser, 1973); time spent with child on activities which aid cognitive development (Leibowitz, 1977); imparting values, aspirations and motivation needed to succeed in school (Wright and Wright, 1976); good communication between parents and children (Dornbusch *et al.*, 1987).

4.2.2 Parental interest and support

Although a number of studies (for example Fehrmann *et al*, 1987) have found a link between parental interest and support and achievement, there is some evidence that parental interest and support (in terms of the number of parent-school contacts and satisfaction with the school) tended to decline as their children progressed through the secondary school (West *et al*, 1992). Wedge and Prosser (1973) found that parents in disadvantaged areas had less frequent contacts with their children's schools than those in more advantaged areas. However, both Wedge and Prosser (op. cit.) and Halsey (1972) found evidence of high parental interest and aspirations for their children in disadvantaged areas, although this did not seem to be translated into higher staying on rates.

4.2.3 Poverty

Research suggests that poverty is associated with low achievement. For example a study carried out in Buckinghamshire over a 12-year period found that poverty was linked with low achievement in reading (Neustatter, 1991). Other research has shown that poor nutrition adversely affects neurological growth and brain efficiency. Lynne (1991) described a study involving over a million children in New York which suggested that improvements in the nutritional quality of school lunches 'assisted' with a 13 per cent rise in educational standards. There is also well-documented evidence that poverty can lead to ill health (McEvaddy 1988).

There is also evidence of a link between poverty and absenteeism. The Elton Report (1989) cited research evidence (Galloway *et al*, 1985) showing that Year 10 and Year 11 pupils from families which were badly housed and which had a multiplicity of economic, social and health problems were more likely to be persistent truants than pupils who were less disadvantaged.

Poverty can also have an adverse effect on children's self-esteem and aspirations (Bradshaw, 1990; Mar-Molinero, 1992): for example lack of fashionable clothes and toys, lack of a suitable place to do homework, less likelihood of parental involvement in their schooling. A primary school headteacher interviewed by Neustatter (op. cit.) stressed that 'policy makers...seem blind to the effects of poverty - malnutrition and hunger, bad health, lack of peace and privacy at home...and to the very real handicap which poor children suffer in the classroom.'

Poverty can also have an adverse effect at school level. Poor parents are less likely to have the energy and confidence to become involved in their children's school (as parent governors or in fund raising). Mar-Molinero (op. cit.) argues that open enrolment is likely to exacerbate the problems of schools in poor areas, since the more aspiring parents living there will opt for higher achieving schools in more affluent areas.

There is evidence that the number of children living in poverty has doubled during the past decade and inequalities have grown wider (Bradshaw, 1990). The above findings therefore suggest that there is clearly cause for concern.

4.3   Student-related factors

4.3.1   Boredom and disaffection

Research suggests that boredom could well be a precursor of disaffection. Entwistle (1988) cites research in Scotland (Gow and McPherson, 1980; Sharp and Thompson, 1984) which found that 'boredom, was the term most frequently used by low achieving pupils when complaining about their experiences at school'. Similarly, Robinson (1990), in interviews carried out with some of the most anti-school students in the first five years of three schools, found that boredom with school was the most frequently mentioned factor. The main reason given for boredom was the inability to understand lessons. He argues that it is probable that certain students in England become more and more bored as they move up the school, and that once students have lost interest, they will look for ways (such as chattering or disruptive behaviour in class) in order to alleviate boredom.

Interestingly, in a study reported by Kysel *et al.* (1992), enjoyment of school work was given as a reason for staying on by some 30 per cent of the students who planned to continue their education beyond the statutory leaving age.

4.3.2   Dislike of teachers and disaffection

Bealing (1990) reported that one of the main reasons given by students for disliking school was dislike of certain teachers or types of teachers, and, in a study reported in Weston (1990), students' relationships with teachers figured strongly in their comments about what they did not like about school.

4.3.3   Achievement and attitudes towards school and learning

Research evidence suggests that there is a significant association between poor achievement and disaffection, but the direction of causality, if any, is not clear. It could be argued that disaffection results from poor achievement (Veerman, 1987). Alternatively, disaffection could be regarded as a causal factor in poor achievement in which case strategies designed to improve motivation to learn will also improve achievement. It seem probable that, whatever the starting point, poor achievement reinforces disaffection and disaffection reinforces poor achievement. A similar relationship may exist between positive attitudes and high achievement (Aiken 1970).

However, a more detailed examination of the research literature on the associations between students' attitudes towards school or education and achievement suggests that the strength of the association varies depending on the attitude dimension under consideration. In the following discussion, therefore, each attitude dimension will be examined separately.

Achievement and liking for school: the associations between students' liking for school and achievement appear to be weak or non-existent. Keys (1987), for example, found very little correlation between liking for school and science achievement amongst primary and secondary school students, and Ainley and Bourke (1992) found no associations between their general satisfaction scale (enjoyment of school) and mathematics and reading achievement amongst top primary school pupils.

Achievement and attitudes towards school work: a large number of studies have identified low but statistically significant positive associations bwteen attitudes towards science and science achievement (Omerod with Duckworth, 1975; Gardner, 1975; Keys, 1978, 1987; Foxman, 1992). Similarly, several studies have demonstrated positive associations between attitudes towards mathematics and mathematics attainment (Foxman *et al.*, 1991; Foxman, 1992). In the international study reported by Foxman (op. cit.), positive associations between attitudes and attainment in science were found in 15 of the 20 countries and for mathematics in 11 of the 12 countries. Positive associations were also found in an Assessment of Performance Unit (APU) study between attitudes towards French and achievement in French (Dickson *et al.*, 1987).

Achievement and educational aspirations: measures concerned with students' educational aspirations have been found to be positively associated with achievement. Keys (1978, 1987), found weak positive associations between measures of educational aspirations and science achievement amongst secondary school pupils and Ainsworth and Baten (1974) found similar associations for mathematics.

Achievement and self-esteem: research evidence suggests that poor self-esteem is associated with low achievement and high self-esteem with high achievement. Brookover *et al.* (1967), for example, showed that the academic performance of high school students improved when they were encouraged to believe that they could do better at school, and Lacey (1970) concluded that the performance and behaviour of grammar school boys who were placed in the lowest stream deteriorated as a result of lowered self-esteem and consequent rejection of the school's values. Similarly, Carr *et al.*, (1991) and Ainley and Bourke (1992) found an association between poor self-esteem and low achievement. There is some evidence that the self-esteem of low achieving students in England is lower than that of their counterparts in other countries. In a comparison of the correlates of achievement in England, France and Japan carried out in the late 1980s, Robinson (1990) found that low achieving students in England showed poorer levels of self-esteem than similar pupils in the other two countries.

4.3.4 Age-related differences in attitudes

One of the hypotheses being tested by the NFER study was that students' motivation towards school and learning is lower in Year 9 than in Year 7. A study reported by Igoe and Sullivan (1991) confirmed this hypothesis. In a study of about 400 students in one high school in the US, they found that Grade 9 students, compared with those in Grade 7, took less responsibility for their learning, desired less personal challenge, cared less about the approval of others and felt less school-related competence. Brighouse (1992) found similar age-related differences amongst much larger samples of students in England.

4.3.5 Gender-related differences in attitudes

Many studies have found that girls tend to hold more positive attitudes towards school than do boys (Igoe and Sullivan, 1991; Ainley and Bourke, 1992). On the other hand, there is evidence that boys, on average, tend to have higher self-esteem than girls (reference).

Comparisons concerned with attitudes towards school subjects appear to depend upon the subject concerned: for example studies of attitudes towards science have generally found that boys held more positive attitudes than girls (Ormerod with Duckworth, 1975; Keys, 1987) whereas those of attitudes towards modern foreign languages have reported that girls' attitudes were more positive than those of boys (Dickson *et al.*, 1987).

4.3.6 Ethnic differences

We have not, so far, been able to find any research directly comparing the motivation towards school of different ethnic groups. However, several studies have compared the performance of different ethnic groups in public examinations. Drew and Gray (1990), for example, used data from the Youth Cohort Study to compare Afro-Caribbean, Asian and white students in terms of examination performance at 16-plus. A drawback of using a nationally representative sample of 16-year-olds to make comparisons between ethnic groups is that the proportion of ethnic minority students in the 16-plus age-group as a whole is very low (about five per cent) and, hence, even with a very large sample (about 14,000), the actual number of ethnic minority students in the sample will be very small (about 700). On the other hand, the use of a national sample makes the results more generalisable than those from a study carried out in a single district.

Drew and Gray (op. cit.) found that 21 per cent of the white students and 19 per cent of the Asian students achieved five or more CSE 1 or O (A/C) passes, compared with only seven per cent of the Afro-Caribbean students. However, when ethnic comparisons were made within socio-economic group, based on parental occupation (i.e. 'like was compared with like' in terms of socio-economic status), the differences between ethnic groups became much smaller. This suggests that some of the variation in achievement between ethnic groups can be explained by socio-economic status.

Kysel (1988) reports comparisons made by ILEA, using 1985 public examination data on 17,000 students in 106 ILEA maintained secondary schools. Since the proportion of ethnic minority students in ILEA was much larger than the proportion for England and Wales as a whole, Kysel (op. cit.) was able to use more detailed ethnic categories than were Drew and Gray (op. cit.). Kysel (op. cit.) reports that 26 per cent of Indian students, 25 per cent of African Asian students and 18 per cent of Bangladeshi students achieved five or more CSE 1 or O (A/C) passes, compared with only five per cent of Caribbean, ten per cent of African and ten per cent of English/Scottish/Welsh/Irish (ESWI).

Even allowing for errors of measurement and differences in classification systems between the two studies, the proportion of ESWI students achieving higher grade passes in ILEA was less than half the proportion gaining similar qualifications in the Youth Cohort Study (which was representative of the whole population in England and Wales). In considering ways of combating the low achievement of some ethnic minority students, it would clearly be unwise to ignore the problem of low achievement amongst the white majority in inner city areas.

Nevertheless, it is possible that racial discrimination may play a part in the underachievement of ethnic minority students. The Swann Report (1985), quoted in Demaine (1989) argued that:

> *School performance has long been known to show a close correlation with socio-economic status and social class, in the case of all children. The ethnic minorities, however, are particularly disadvantaged in social and economic terms, and there can no longer be any doubt that this extra deprivation is the result of racial prejudice and discrimination, especially in the areas of employment and housing. This extra deprivation, over and above that of disadvantaged Whites, leads in many cases to an extra element of underachievement.*

Underachievement amongst ethnic minority students may, in some cases be due to lack of fluency in English. For example there have been suggestions that poor achievement on the recent pilot National Assessment in science amongst ethnic minority students is the result of lack of fluency in English rather than lack of understanding of science (Skelton, 1992) and Kysel (1988) cite the ILEA Language Census findings showing that only 22 per cent of fifth-year Bengali-speaking students were rated as fully fluent in English by their teachers. Yet, schools in inner city areas frequently report that they have insufficient resources to address their students' language problems in the way they would wish.

We have been unable to find many studies relating attitudes and behaviour to ethnic minority membership. However, the study of 12 inner London schools reported by Rutter *et al* (1979) found that there was a significant correlation between the proportion of pupils from ethnic minority (mainly West Indian) homes and school delinquency rates, but not with truancy rates, other pupil behaviour measures or attainment.

4.4 School and teaching factors related to motivation

Our examination of the relevant research literature suggests that certain school and teaching factors, sometimes described collectively as 'school ethos' or 'school climate', are systematically associated with pupils' attitudes towards school and education and with their behaviour in school.

In their brief review of the literature, Rutter *et al*. (1979) concluded that 'schools differ on a variety of quite different features and there are strong suggestions that differences may have an important influence on the children's behaviour and scholastic progress. The possibly relevant features include the amount of teaching and degree of academic emphasis, the extent and nature of ability groupings, teacher expectations, styles of teaching and classroom management, the size of the school, patterns of discipline and the characteristics of overall school climate or atmosphere...but so far research results allow few firm conclusions'.

Their own study, which is sub-titled *Secondary Schools and their Effects on Children,* goes a long way towards remedying this deficiency. It examines the relationship between school factors and pupils' attendance, attainment and behaviour. Most of the main conclusions of their study confirm previous research but, because of the large size and high quality of the research, they enable us to draw firmer conclusions than was previously the case. These conclusions are summarised below:

- Secondary schools in inner London differed markedly in the behaviour and attainments of their pupils.

- Differences between schools on various 'outcome' measures were stable over time.

- Schools with high attainment also tended to have good attendance and well-behaved pupils (i.e. there were high correlations between the three outcome variables).

- Differences in outcomes did not appear to be due to physical factors of the schools, such as size or condition of buildings.

- Differences between schools were systematically related to their characteristics as social institutions (degree of academic emphasis, teaching approaches, incentives and rewards, the extent to which pupils were given responsibility).

- The associations between the combined measure of school process and each of the outcome measures were stronger than any of the associations with individual school process measures.

- The associations between school process and outcomes is probably partially causal.

In addition, several of their findings extend previous research in a useful way:

- Differences in outcome could not wholly be explained by differences in school intake.

- The effect of the balance of intake was most marked with respect to delinquency (schools with a high proportion of less able children tended to have relatively high levels of delinquency).

Further evidence of the importance of school-related factors in determining pupils attitudes and behaviour comes from a study of London primary schools carried out by Mortimore *et al.* (1988), who found that school membership explained 8 - 12 per cent of the variation in pupils' attitudes towards school and school subjects (this was larger than the proportion explained by background factors, sex or age). They also found that school membership made a significant, though not dominant, contribution to the explanation of differences in pupils' behaviour (ten per cent), and that it had a small effect on levels of attendance (where it explained about six per cent of the variation) and on pupils' self-concept (about eight per cent).

Weindling (1989) has identified, from these and other studies, a number of factors which have tended to be associated with effective schools. The list of factors below has been developed from Weindling's work, supplemented by additional factors identified by Mortimore *et al.* (1988), Branwhite (1988), Caffyn (1989), Brophy (1987), and Entwistle and Ramsden (1983).

> *School management:* clear goals; positive leadership by the head and senior management team (American studies use the term 'instructional leadership', which is the attention the head pays to classroom instruction and learning and the amount of classroom observation by the head); teacher involvement in curriculum planning; consistency amongst teachers; school-wide staff development which is closely related to the curriculum; buildings kept in good order.

Academic emphasis: high academic expectations by teachers; regular homework; visible rewards for academic excellence and growth.

Continual monitoring of students' progress: school-wide monitoring policy.

Effective discipline and rule enforcement: whole-school policy which links incentives directly with good social behaviour and academic performance.

Classroom management: high proportion of lesson time spent on the subject matter of the lesson (as distinct from setting up equipment, dealing with disciplinary matters, etc.); limited focus within sessions; intellectually challenging teaching; high proportion of teacher time spent interacting with the class as a whole as opposed to individuals; lessons beginning and ending on time; clear explanations; clear and unambiguous feedback to students on their performance and what is expected of them; ample praise for good performance; continual monitoring of students' progress; minimum disciplinary interventions.

External support: LEA/district support; parental involvement and support.

Factors such as pupil-teacher ratio, overall expenditure on resources and salaries; school size, class size and organisational structure have not been found to be closely associated with school effectiveness. We also examined some of the research literature on the school-based factors associated with suspensions, disruptive behaviour, truancy and dropout.

A study by McManus (1987) into the associations between suspension or exclusion and catchment/school variables in 49 secondary schools in Leeds provides an interesting insight. Using regression analysis, McManus found that three school factors explained half the variation in school suspension rates and that each factor alone explained more than catchment as represented by free school meals. These were: the degree to which form tutors took responsibility for their group's discipline in school; the type of support provision for disruptive pupils; the number of offences regarded as meriting suspension; and to a lesser extent the way senior staff dealt with the troublesome classes reported to them.

Interestingly, a survey of teachers' attitudes towards disruptive behaviour in secondary schools (Maxwell, 1987) found that teachers tended to see factors in the home as the most important causes of disruptive behaviour. However, they believed that school-based strategies (such as in-service training in class-management skills, greater pastoral care input and better liaison with outside agencies) were most likely to reduce disruptive behaviour. The analysis of staff attitudes revealed significant differences between schools in the extent to which staff believed that the problem of disruptive behaviour was within the power of the school to control.

In a study of absenteeism in one secondary school Bealing (1990) found that pupils generally gave school-based reasons for truanting. Boredom created by uninteresting lessons and ineffective teachers was the most frequent reason given for missing lessons. Pupils indicated that it was relatively easy to miss lessons ('post-registration' truancy) since the school encouraged resource based learning. However, pupils described activities undertaken during 'post-registration' absenteeism as not particularly interesting or enjoyable (sitting in the toilets, talking and smoking), although better than lessons. On the other hand, whole days spent truanting (shopping trips, meals at friends' houses, part-time work, watching videos and staying in bed) were described as much more enjoyable. Although interesting, it should be borne in mind that this study was concerned with a single school.

CHAPTER 5
STRATEGIES TO IMPROVE STUDENTS' MOTIVATION, BEHAVIOUR, ACHIEVEMENTS & FUTURE PROSPECTS

5.1   School improvement schemes

In *The Times Educational Supplement*/Annual Greenwich Lecture, Mortimore (1991) points out that, although much of the research into school effectiveness (some of which is reported in Section 4.4 of this review) has taken place in the United Kingdom, we have so far failed to implement any large-scale school improvement schemes which make use of the findings of research into school effectiveness.   In North America, on the other hand, a number of school improvement schemes have been implemented (many of those in the United States with public funding).   Mortimore's (op. cit.) brief description of two of these schemes is reproduced below:

> *One distinctive approach to American school improvement is that of James Comer, a child psychiatrist who, since 1968, has worked with schools to improve the relationships between teachers, pupils and parents in order to facilitate learning (Comer, 1991). His nine-component model integrated within an overall school development plan has...been awarded a five year $15 million grant from the Rockefeller Foundation. His approach accepts that children and young people in urban areas undergo stressful experiences and that schools need to find ways of diverting the energy, caused by these stresses, into learning.   All the schools using his methods also adopt development plans and build in high levels of parental involvement.*

> *Another approach has been pioneered in Ontario by the Halton School Board (Stoll and Fink, 1988). Based on Britain and American research, this approach to school improvement focuses on the creation, by a school team, of a school growth plan.   This growth plan incorporated an assessment of each school's strengths and weaknesses; a vision of how a team would like to see the school develop; specific plans of how to move towards the vision; and a built in evaluation programme to provide feedback on progress. The school teams are assisted by academics from the University of Toronto and by researchers and consultants from the district office who specialise in evaluation techniques.*

5.2. Pre-school intervention strategies

5.2.1 The Head Start movement in the United States

Project Head Start was initiated in 1965 as an experimental six-week summer programme to provide child developmental services to low-income families of pre-school children in the United States. Programmes have since increased in length and now normally operate for nine months or a full-year. In the late 1980s, over 450,000 children were enrolled on Head Start programmes each year and the annual budget was more than one billion dollars. The programmes were operated by about 1300 community-based non-profit making agencies (Nielsen, 1989).

The overall aim of Head Start is to develop in the child a greater everyday effectiveness in dealing both with present environment and later responsibilities in school and life.

The pre-school curricula adopted by Head Start programmes vary and include: traditional moderately structured nursery school approaches; highly structured curricula based on behaviour modification techniques; cognitive curricula based on Piagetian theory; and the Montessori approach. In addition to pre-school education, Head Start programmes also offer free or low cost medical and dental services to the children, education for parents on hygiene and nutrition, a variety of other health education schemes, schemes to involve grandparents in their grandchildren's education and adult literacy provision (Nielsen, 1989).

Research into the outcomes of Head Start programmes have shown that one year later, Head Start children outperform non-Head Start children on achievement and school readiness tests, but, in many cases these advantages have been found to disappear over time (Nielsen, 1989).

However, there is some evidence that children who have attended Head Start schemes are more likely to function better as adult members of a community than those who had not. Jowett and Sylva (1988), for example, cited American research (Berruetta-Clement *et al.*, 1984) which found that children who had attended the Perry Pre-school Project were more likely to graduate from high school, to enrol in college and to be employed than those who had not attended.

There is a suggestion that pre-school intervention needs to be followed up in subsequent years if it is to be effective: Nielsen (1989) cites other research which shows that when Head Start experiences are followed by a Follow Through programme, which continually builds on earlier Head Start experience, Head Start children maintain their advantages in comparison with their non-Head Start peers (Borden *et al.*, 1975).

5.2.2 The Educational Priority Area Projects (EPA) in the United Kingdom

The EPA projects were set up in 1968 as a result of the recommendations of the Plowden Report 1967 for an inquiry into the educational needs of inner city areas. The brief of the EPA project was to undertake pilot action with a view to recommending a national policy for socially disadvantaged areas (Midwinter, 1972).

The EPA project, which was funded for three years, consisted of five projects in different areas of the United Kingdom: Birmingham, Liverpool, London, Oxford and the West Riding. The main recommendations of the EPA Project were summed up by Halsey (1972) as follows:

> These limits (of an educational approach to poverty) cannot be removed by any kind of EPA policy. But within them we think we can see a viable road to a higher standard of educational living for hundreds of thousands of children in the more disadvantaged districts.

> We have outlined a wide range of policies around the development of pre-schooling and the community school, and we have called for a coordinated advance of statutory and voluntary effort. The action research project method, adroitly constituted to work with 'the system' but with a small but essential element of independence from the normal administrative procedures, has proved itself to be an effective agent of educational change and a magnet for voluntary effort from a wide range of public and private organisations. Such projects, perhaps linked in some cases to the current Community Development Projects, could carry forward the development of EPA policy as we have done in three years from its inception in the Plowden Report. At the same time we would hope that there is sufficient confidence in our results from the first projects for the Government and the local education authorities to create the framework of organisation for pre-schooling and community schooling that we have advocated. If so there will be a new landmark in British educational progress.

The percentage of three-year-olds in maintained nursery schools and classes has increased since 1970 (from 4 per cent in 1970 to 37 per cent in 1991 almost entirely because of an expansion in part-time enrolments (DES Statistical Bulletins 9/87 and 5/92). However, community education, as recommended by the EPA project, hardly exists at all. Perhaps the last word should be given to Eric Midwinter who, in 1972, wrote:

> My own social historical guess is that a completed and perfected pattern of community education will, on present trends, take between fifty and a hundred years to achieve. My instincts tell me that this may be too little

too late. Certainly I am convinced that, over the next decades, the concept of community education will be one of the foremost issues facing teachers and schools; it could be the most dramatic challenge that the public education system has faced in a hundred years.

5.3 Primary school intervention strategies

5.3.1 The Reading Recovery Scheme

The Reading Recovery Scheme (Clay, 1972) is used throughout New Zealand, where it was developed, in three Australian states, three Canadian provinces and 41 American States. It is already being used by Surrey LEA and the DFE is spending about £3 million on ESGs to put the scheme into inner-city areas (Dean, 1992).

The scheme identifies any six-year-old who has not 'taken off' in reading and gives him a short burst of individual, intensive help for half an hour a day to bring him back to the average level for his age. Help is given initially to the four poorest readers in a class, and once they have caught up, the process is repeated with the next poorest until the whole class has achieved an acceptable standard. In New Zealand 99 per cent of children 'catch up' within 12 to 20 weeks. (Moore, 1991).

Reading Recovery is relatively costly in terms of resources: one year's part-time training for the teacher; supply cover during training; teacher time to provide half an hour of one-to-one teaching for four pupils each day plus time to complete records and plan courses - about half a full-time equivalent teacher (Moore, 1991).

However, it appears to be successful: according to Professor Clay, follow-up studies in Ohio and New Zealand showed that gains made by students were maintained three years later (Dean, 1992). How far this success was due to the scheme itself and how far it was due to the greatly increased resources devoted to the students concerned is impossible to say.

5.4   Secondary school intervention strategies

5.4.1   The Technical and Vocational Education Initiative (TVEI)

The aim of TVEI was to change the curriculum experienced by 14 to 18-year-olds by giving their education a more practical, applied and relevant focus. TVEI is not a course of study nor is it concerned solely with technical and vocational skills. The original pilot projects varied in size and scope. The main outcomes of TVEI are summarised briefly below:

On the plus side, TVEI was successful in:

- establishing new courses of a more practical and vocational nature (such as business studies, technology, agriculture, caring, catering and creative arts);

- encouraging links between the subject matter taught in class and applications in the outside world;

- promoting developments in modular course structures and assessment, changes in teaching styles and collaboration between institutions;

- although research comparing TVEI and non-TVEI students in terms of examination success has been inconclusive, there is evidence that TVEI students were more likely to obtain employment than non-TVEI students in the same schools.

On the minus side:

- short planning time-scales in the pilot phase led to some unfocused work and a waste of resources;

- the original restriction of TVEI enhancement to a maximum of 50 students per school per year caused hostility form teachers and students not involved;

- the early pilot phases were not successful in increasing participation on post-16 education and training.

(Great Britain. DES, 1991).

5.4.2 Records of Achievement (RoA)

In 1984, the DES issued a policy statement on Records of Achievement. Development work was undertaken in 22 LEAs in England and Wales. Once these schemes had been evaluated, it was intended that all schools would operate a Records of Achievement scheme. The main purposes of Records of Achievement were:

● recognition of achievement - the acknowledgement of all aspects of a student's achievement and experiences in school as well as public examination successes;

● motivation and personal development - the improvement of motivation through increasing awareness of strengths, weaknesses and opportunities;

● curriculum organisation - helping schools to match the curriculum to the all-round potential of their students;

● a document of record - students leaving school or college should take with them a short, summary record of their achievements.

TVEI schemes now require participating students to have some form of RoA, although there is no statutory obligation on all schools to operate a scheme for other students (Weston, 1990).

5.4.3 The Lower Attaining Pupils Programme (LAPP)

The Lower Attaining Pupils Programme, which began in 1983 in 13 LEAs and was extended to four more LEAs two years later, sponsored LEA initiatives aimed at meeting the needs of the broad range of students who had traditionally performed poorly in public examinations at the age of 16. It involved a whole range of innovations in assessment systems and approaches for 14 to16 year-olds. The schemes were of two main types: two-year courses with their own qualifications, either as lower level options in the usual school subjects or in special schemes of prevocational studies; short modules or units, usually lasting from a few weeks to two months, each with its own certificate, which could be combined in a variety of ways as part of each student's total curriculum. The majority of schemes were developed by teams of teachers working locally. Generally, they included practical activities and short-term learning targets, involved students in planning and evaluating their own work, and used non-traditional methods of assessing students' work (Weston, 1990).

5.4.4 Compact

The Compacts initiative, funded by the Employment Department from 1988, has the main aim of raising attainment of young people in education, training and work by guaranteeing a job with training for all young people aged 14 and over who meet their personal goals.

Each Compact is a contract between employers, school, colleges, training providers and young people, where each party makes a commitment to achieve agreed goals such as:

- schools, colleges and training providers work with young people to improve levels of achievement;

- young people make a commitment to attending school regularly and to completing their coursework on time and to the best of their ability;

- employers agree to provide jobs with training, or training leading to a job, for young people who achieve their goals.

Compacts are normally based in Urban Programme Authority areas in England and priority areas in Scotland and Wales.

5.4.5 Pre-vocational education and training in Europe

A paper by Stradling (1991), describes a number of pre-vocational education and training schemes in Europe. The main schemes described by Stradling (op. cit.) are listed below.

Belgium: Alternating Education, which is partially funded by the European Social Fund, and involves both employers and the education service, is a two-year scheme which provides part-time work linked to practical skills-based part-time education.

Spain: Workshop School and Craft Centres provide training places for up to 30,000 young people, mostly poorly qualified unemployed school leavers. The scheme, which is of three years duration, provides training linked to part-time work on local developments, particularly in the area of cultural heritage and the environment.

Denmark: pilot projects, involving multi-disciplinary coordinating groups, have been set up to provide guidance and training programmes for school leavers and young unemployed.

France: the 'Missions Locales', which are funded equally by local and national government, provide a similar service to the Danish groups.

Ireland: the YOUTHREACH programme, which is subsidised by the ESF, guarantees up to two years of coordinated education, training and work experience for unqualified unemployed early school leavers.

The
Netherlands: small-scale experimental projects, which are designed to remotivate school dropouts, have been set up.

CHAPTER 6
SUMMARY AND CONCLUSIONS

i.   Motivation has been described as the drive to succeed. Motivation towards school and education has been explained in several different ways. It may be intrinsic (arising from interest in the subject being studied) or extrinsic (depending on the availability of external rewards). It may arise from a need to achieve or from fear of failure: a student who has failed or fears to fail at school may safeguard his self-esteem by redirecting his efforts away from school towards more easily attained goals. Such a student could be described as disaffected or disengaged from school.

ii.   Disruptive behaviour, truancy and early leaving are often seen as outcomes of disaffection or disengagement from school.

iii.   A common set of negative factors has been found to be associated with disruptive behaviour, truancy and early leaving. These can be divided into three groups: students' attitudes, their achievement and home/societal influences.

Students' attitudes:
- disillusionment with and dislike of school;
- lack of interest and effort in class and homework;
- boredom with school and schoolwork;
- dislike of certain teachers or types of teachers;
- resentment of school rules;
- belief that school would not improve career prospect;
- low educational aspirations;
- low self-esteem.

Students' achievement:
- poor academic achievement.

Home/societal influences:

- lack of parental interest and support;

- low socio-economic status;

- poverty and sub-standard housing;

- inner city catchment area;

- peer group pressures from anti-school friendship groups.

iv. A set of positive factors, the reverse of some of the negative factors associated with disaffection, was found, in the studies reviewed, to be associated with favourable attitudes towards school and education. These are:

Students' attitudes:

- enjoyment of and interest in school work;

- belief that school qualifications will improve career prospects;

- high educational aspirations

- high self-esteem

Students' achievement:

- high achievement (which appears to be associated with liking for school work but not with liking for school).

Interestingly, the review found very little association between students' attitudes and socio-economic status or any other home/societal factors.

v. Two studies were found which confirmed the Working Group's hypotheses that students' motivation towards school and learning is lower in Year 9 than in Year 7.

vi. Research involving a nationally representative sample suggests that Afro-Caribbean students under-perform in public examinations at 16-plus compared with White and Asian students. Research carried out in ILEA schools, however, found that white students in inner city schools, as well as Africans and Caribbeans, under-performed as compared with Asians.

vii. It has been suggested that the under-achievement of some ethnic minority students can be explained by lack of fluency in English and, that, in general, schools are not able to devote adequate resources to tackle this problem.

viii. Our examination of the relevant research literature suggests that certain school and teaching factors, sometimes described collectively as 'school ethos' or 'school climate', are systematically associated with pupils' attitudes towards school and education and with their behaviour in school. These factors are:

- effective school management: clear goals; positive leadership; teacher involvement in curriculum planning; school-wide staff development policy;

- academic emphasis: regular homework; rewards for academic excellence;

- regular monitoring of students' progress;

- effective school-wide discipline and rule enforcement;

- effective classroom management: high proportion of lesson time spent on subject matter; intellectually challenging teaching; clear explanations; positive feedback; good discipline;

- external support: LEA/district support; parental involvement and support.

Factors such as pupil-teacher ratio, overall expenditure on resources and salaries, school size, class size and organisational structure have not been found to be closely associated with school effectiveness.

ix. During the last 20 - 30 years, a number of strategies have been developed in the United Kingdom, the United States and Europe which attempt to counteract poor achievement and disaffection and to improve the life chances of underachieving and/or socially disadvantaged students. These schemes have focused on:

- pre-school education complemented with free or subsidised health care for children and health education for parents (Head Start);

- pre-school education and community schools (the EPA project);

- remedial intervention in the infant school (Reading Recovery scheme);

- work-related curriculum development in the secondary school (TVEI, LAPP, Compact);

The research reviewed suggests that most of these schemes have had some measure of success. Many have been, at least in part, Government-funded. Most have been costly in terms of resources and have required the participation and support of enthusiastic, well-trained and effective teachers.

x.   In conclusion, it seems clear from the research examined by this review that a number of factors which could be changed by schools are associated with disengagement from school and learning. Furthermore, most of the previous and existing strategies designed to improve motivation towards school and learning and subsequent life chances of disaffected or underachieving pupils have had some success. This suggests that future strategies, either similar to those described above or based on the findings of this review, would have a good chance of achieving some measure of success. However, it is unlikely that such strategies will succeed unless they are adequately resourced in terms of funding, staff training and staff time.

xi.   Furthermore, this review has identified a number of societal and home background factors (poverty, poor housing, low socio-economic status and lack of parental support) which are strongly associated with poor achievement, disaffection, disruption, truancy and early leaving and which cannot easily, if at all, be changed by the school. These factors will need to be addressed. It seems clear that, on its own, as Bernstein (1970) wrote, *Education cannot compensate for society.*

REFERENCES

AINLEY, J. and BOURKE, S. (1992). 'Student views of primary schooling', *Research Papers in Education*, **7**, 2, 107-28.

AIKEN, L. (1970). 'Attitudes towards mathematics', *Review of Educational Research*, **40**, 551-96.

AINSWORTH, M.M. and BATEN, E.J. (1974). *The Effects of Environmental Factors on Secondary Educational Attainment in Mathematics: a Plowden Follow-up*. London: Macmillan.

BEALING, V. (1990). 'Inside information', *Maladjustment and Therapeutic Education*, **8**, 1, 19-34.

BERNSTEIN, B. (1970). 'Education cannot compensate for society', *New Society*, **387**, February.

BERRUETA-CLEMENT, J.R., SCHWEINHART, L.J., BARNETT, S., EPSTEIN, A. and WEIKART, D. (1984). *Changed Lives: the Effects of the Perry Preschool Programme on Youths Through Age 19* (Monographs of the High/Scope Educational Research Foundation, No.8). Ypsilanti, Michigan: The High/Scope Press.

BLATCHFORD, P. (1992). 'Children's attitudes to work at 11 years', *Educational Studies*, **18**, 1, 107-18.

BORDEN, J.P., HANDLEY, H.M. and WOLLENBERG, J.P. (1975). 'Extended effects of a comprehensive Head Start - follow through program sequences on academic performance of rural disadvantged children', *Journal of Negro Education*, **44**, 149-69.

BRADSHAW, J. (1990). *Child Poverty and Deprivation in the UK*. London: National Children's Bureau.

BRANWHITE, T. (1988). 'The Pass Survey: school-based preferences of 500+ adolescent consumers', *Educational Studies*, **14**, 2, 165-76.

BRIGHOUSE, T. (1992). Address to the National Commission on Education Conference, Manchester, 13 July (unpublished).

BROOKOVER, W.B., ERICKSON, E. and JOINER, M. (1967). *Self-Concept of Ability and School Achievement 111*. East Lansing: Michigan College of Education, Michigan State University.

BROPHY, J. (1987). 'Socializing student motivation to learn.' In: MAEHR, M.L. and KLEIBER, E.A. (Eds) *Advances in Motivation and Achievement* (Volume 5). Greenwich, CT: JAI Press.

CAFFYN, R.E. (1989). 'Attitudes of British secondary school teachers and pupils to rewards and punishments', *Educational Research*, **31**, 3, 210-20.

CARR, M., BORKOWSKI, J.G. and MAXWELL, S.E. (1991). 'Motivational components of underachievement', *Developmental Psychology*, **27**, 1, 108-18.

CLAY, M.J. (1972). *The Early Detection of Reading Difficulties: a Diagnostic Survey*. Auckland: Heinemann.

COLEMAN, J.S., CAMPBELL, E.Q., HOBSON, C.J., McPARTLAND, J., MOOD, A.M., WEINFELD, F. and YORK, R.L. (1966). *Equality of Educational Opportunity*. Washington DC: US Government Printing Office.

COMBER, L.C. and KEEVES J.P. (1973). *Science Education in Nineteen Countries*. Stockholm, Almqvist and Wiksell

COMER, J. (1991). 'The Comer School Development Programme', *Urban Education* **26**, 1, 56-82.

CROXFORD, L. and McPHERSON, A. (in press) *School Leavers in Glasgow and its Areas of Registration*. Edinburgh: Edinburgh University Centre for Educational Sociology.

CUTTANCE, P. (1980). 'Do schools consistently influence the performance of their students?' *Educational Review*, **32**, 3, 267-80.

DEAN, C. (1992). 'Reading rescue act under way', *Times Educational Supplement*, 3941, 10 January, p12.

DEAN, J. (1982a). *Educational Choice at 16: Interim Report* (RS 818/82). London: Inner London Education Authority.

DEAN, J. (1982b). *Educational Choice at 16: Final Report* (RS 835/82). London: Inner London Education Authority.

DEMAINE, J. (1989). 'Race, categorisation and educational achievement'. *British Journal of Sociology of Education*, **10**, 2, 195-214,

DICKSON, P., BOYCE, C., LEE, B., PORTAL, M. and SMITH, M. (1987). *Foreign Language Performance in Schools. Report on 1985 Survey of French* (APU Survey). London: HMSO.

DORNBUSCH, S.M., RITTER, P.L., LEIDERMAN, P.H., ROBERTS, D.F. and FRALEIGH, M.J. (1987). 'The relation of parenting style to adolescent school performance', *Child Development*, **58**, 5, 1244-57.

DOUGLAS, T. (1983). *Groups: Understanding People Gathered Together*. London: Tavistock Publications.

DREW, D. and GRAY, J. (1990). 'The fifth-year examination achievements of black young people in England and Wales', *Educational Research*, **32**, 2, 107-17.

EKSTROM, R.B., GOERTZ, M.E., POLLACK, J.M. and ROCK, D.A. (1986). 'Who drops out of high school and why? Findings from a national study'. *Teachers College Record*, **87**, 3, 356-73.

ELTON REPORT. GREAT BRITAIN. DEPARTMENT OF EDUCATION AND SCIENCE. COMMITTEE OF ENQUIRY INTO DISCIPLINE IN SCHOOLS (1989). *Discipline in Schools*. London: HMSO.

ENTWISTLE, N. (1988). 'Research on motivation to learn.' In: SCOTTISH COUNCIL FOR RESEARCH IN EDUCTION (1988). *Motivation in Education. What Role for Research?* (Forum on Educational Research in Scotland, Third Meeting, 20 November, 1987). Edinburgh: Scottish Council for Research in Education.

ENTWISTLE, N. and KOZEKI, B. (1985). 'Relationships between school motivation, approaches to studying, and attainment among British and Hugarian adolescents', *British Journal of Educational Psychology*, **55**, 2, 124-37.

ENTWISTLE, N. and KOZEKI, B. (1988). 'Dimensions of motivation and approaches to learning in British and Hungarian secondary schools', *International Journal of Educational Research*, **12**, 3, 243-55.

ENTWISTLE, N. and RAMSDEN, P. (1983). *Understanding Student Learning*. London: Croom Helm.

FEHRMANN, P.G., KEITH, T.Z. and REIMERS, T.M. (1987). 'Home influence on school learning: direct and indirect effects of parental involvement on high school grades', *Journal of Educational Research*, **80**, 6, 330-37.

FOXMAN, D. (1992). *Learning Mathematics and Science. The Second International Assessment of Educational Progress in England*. Slough: NFER.

FOXMAN, D., RUDDOCK, G., McCALLUM, I. and SCHAGEN, I. (1991). *APU Mathematics Monitoring (Phase 2)*. London: SEAC.

GALLOWAY, D., MARTIN, R. and WILCOX, B. (1985). 'Persistent absence from school and exclusion from school: the predictive power of school and community variables', *British Educational Research Journal*, **11**, 1, 51-61.

GARDNER, P.L. (1975). 'Attitudes to science; a review', *Studies in Science Education*, **2**, 1-41.

GOLDSTEIN, H. (1987). *Multilevel Models in Educational and Social Research*. London: Griffin.

GOW, L. and McPHERSON, A. (1980). *Tell Them From Me*. Aberdeen: Aberdeen University Press.

GRAY, J. and JESSON, D. (1987). 'Exam results and local authority league tables.' In: HARRISON, A. and GRETTON, J. (Eds) *Education & Training UK 1987*. Newbury: Policy Journals.

GRAY, J., McPHERSON, A.F. and RAFFE, D. (1983). *Reconstructions of Secondary Education: Theory, Myth and Practice Since the War*. London: Routledge and Kegan Paul.

GREAT BRITAIN. DEPARTMENT OF EDUCATION AND SCIENCE (1972). *Education: a Framework for Expansion* (Cmnd.5174). London: HMSO.

GREAT BRITAIN. DEPARTMENT OF EDUCATION AND SCIENCE (1982). *A Classification of Local Education Authorities by Additional Educational Needs* (Statistical Bulletin 8/82). London: HMSO.

GREAT BRITAIN. DEPARTMENT OF EDUCATION AND SCIENCE. (1987). *Pupils Under Five Years in Each Local Education Authority in England - January 1986* (Statistical Bulletin 9/87). London: DES.

GREAT BRITAIN. DEPARTMENT OF EDUCATION AND SCIENCE. (1992). *Pupils Under Five Years in Each Local Education Authority in England - January 1991* (Statistical Bulletin 5/92). London: DES.

GREAT BRITAIN. DEPARTMENT OF EDUCATION AND SCIENCE. HER MAJESTY'S INSPECTORATE (1991). *Technical and Vocational Education Initiative (TVEI) England and Wales 1983-90*. London: HMSO.

GREAT BRITAIN. DEPARTMENT OF EDUCATION AND SCIENCE. HER MAJESTY's INSPECTORATE (1990). *Standards in Education 1988-1989; the Annual Report of HM Senior Chief Inspector of Schools*. London: DES.

GREAT BRITAIN. DEPARTMENT OF EDUCATION AND SCIENCE. HER MAJESTY'S INSPECTORATE (1991). *Standards in Education 1989-90: the Annual Report of HM Senior Chief Inspector of Schools*. London: DES.

GREAT BRITAIN. DEPARTMENT OF EDUCATION AND SCIENCE. HER MAJESTY'S INSPECTORATE (1992). *Education in England 1990-91: the Annual Report of HM Senior Chief Inspector of Schools.* London: DES.

HALSEY, A.H. (Ed) (1972). *Educational Priority. Volume 1: EPA. Problems and Policies.* London: HMSO.

IGOE, A.R. and SULLIVAN, H. (1991). Gender and grade-level differences in student attributes related to school learning and motivation. Paper presented at the Annual Meeting of the American Educational Research Association, Chicago, IL, 3-7 April.

JENCKS, C., SMITH, M., ACLAND, H., BANE, M.J., COHEN, D., GINTIS, H., HEYNS, B. and MICHELSON, S. (1972). *Inequality: a Reassessment of the Effect of Family and Schooling in America.* New York: Basic Books.

JOWETT, S. and SYLVA, K. (1988). 'On the right track', *Child Education,* **65**, 1, 12-14.

KEYS, W. (1978). Some cognitive, affective and personality correlates of subject bias amongst able English boys and girls in the middle years of secondary education. Unpublished PhD thesis, Brunel University.

KEYS, W. (1987). *Aspects of Science Education in English Schools.* Windsor: NFER-NELSON.

KYSEL, F. (1988). 'Ethnic background and examination results', *Educational Research,* **30**, 2, 83-9.

KYSEL, F., WEST, A. and SCOTT, G. (1992). 'Leaving school: attitudes, aspirations and destinations of fifth-year leavers in Tower Hamlets', *Educational Research,* **34**, 2, 87-105.

LACEY, C. (1970). *Hightown Grammar.* Manchester: Manchester University Press.

LEIBOWITZ, A. (1977). 'Parental inputs and children's achievement'. *Journal of Human Resources,* **12**, 242-51,

LONDON BOROUGH OF NEWHAM (1989). *Boosting Educational Achievement. A Report of an Inquiry into Educational Achievement in the London Borough of Newham* (Chaired by Seamus Hegarty). London: Newham Council Education Committee.

LYNNE, R. (1991). 'Young minds have to be fed', *Times Educational Supplement,* 3896, 1 March, p.20.

MACBEATH, J.E.C. and WEIR, D. (1991). *Attitudes to School: a Digest of UK Surveys and Polls on Parents', Teachers' and Pupils' Attitudes to School 1985-1990*. Glasgow: Jordanhill College of Education.

McEVADDY, S. (1988). *One Good Meal a Day: the Loss of Free School Meals*. London: Child Poverty Action Group.

McMANUS, M. (1987). 'Suspension and exclusion from high schools: the association with catchment and school variables', *Research in Education*, **38**, 51-63.

McPHERSON, A.F. and WILLMS, J.D. (1986). 'Certification, class conflict, religion and community: a socio-historical explanation of the effectiveness of contemporary school.' In: KERCKHOFF, A.C. (Ed) *Research in Sociology of Education and Socialization. Volume 6*. Greenwich, CT: JAI Press.

MAR-MOLINERO, C. (1992). 'Poverty and education', *Forum*, **33**, 2, 55-6.

MAXWELL, W.S. (1987). 'Teachers' attitudes towards disruptive behaviour in secondary schools', *Educational Review*, **39**, 3, 203-16.

MIDWINTER, E. (1972). 'Breaking the vicious circle: the lessons of the Educational Priority Area Projects', *London Educational Review*, **1**, 2, 15-21.

MOORE, G. (1991). 'The road to reading recovery', *Child Education*, **68**, 3, 45-7.

MORTIMORE, P. (1991). Bucking the trends: promoting successful urban education. Times Educational Supplement/Greenwich Annual Lecture at Woolwich Town Hall, November 12.

MORTIMORE, P., SAMMONS, P., STOLL, L., LEWIS, D. and ECOB, R. (1988). *School Matters: the Junior Years*. Wells: Open Books.

MORTON-WILLIAMS, R. and FINCH, S. (1968). *Young School Leavers: Report of a Survey Among Young People, Parents and Teachers (Schools Council Enquiry 1)*. London: HMSO.

NATIONAL COMMISSION ON EDUCATION AND MANCHESTER LEA (1992). *A 13 Years Old's Experience of Education: Research Highlights*. London: National Commission on Education.

NEUSTATTER, A. (1991). 'Hungry to learn', *Times Educational Supplement*, 3914, 5 July, pp 21-2.

NIELSEN, W.L. (1989). 'The longitudinal effects of Project Head Start on students' overall academic success: a review of the literature', *International Journal of Early Childhood*, **21**, 1, 35-42.

ORMEROD, M.B. with DUCKWORTH, D. (1975). *Pupils' Attitudes to Science. A Review of Research*. Windsor: NFER Publishing Company.

OUSTON, J. and MAUGHAN, B. (1985). 'Issues in the assessment of school outcomes.' In: REYNOLDS, D. (Ed) *Studying School Effectiveness*. Lewes: Falmer Press.

PEAKER, G.F. (1971). *The Plowden Children Four Years Later*. Windsor: NFER.

PLOWDEN REPORT. GREAT BRITAIN. DEPARTMENT OF EDUCATION AND SCIENCE. CENTRAL ADVISORY COUNCIL FOR EDUCATION (ENGLAND) (1967). *Children and their Primary Schools*. London: HMSO.

PURKEY, S.C. and SMITH, M.S. (1983). 'Effective schools: a review', *Elementary School Journal*, **83**, 4, 427-52.

RAFFE, D. (1986). 'Unemployment and school motivation: the case of truancy', *Educational Review*, **38**, 1, 11-19.

ROBINSON, W.P. (1990). 'Academic achievement and self-esteem in secondary school: muddles, myths and reality', *Education Research and Perspectives*, **17**, 1, 3-21.

ROLLETT, B. (1987). 'Effort avoidance and learning.' In: DE CORTE, E., LODEWIJKS, H., PARMENTIER, R. and SPAN, P. (Eds) *Learning and Instruction: European Research in an International Context*. Oxford: Pergamon Press.

RUMBERGER, R.W. (1983). 'Dropping out of high school: the influence of race, sex, and family background', *American Educational Research Journal*, **20**, 2, 199-220.

RUMBERGER, R.W. (1987). 'High school dropouts: a review of issues and evidence', *Review of Educational Research*, **57**, 101-21.

RUMBERGER, R.W., GHATAK, R., POULOS, G., RITTER, P.L. and DORNBUSCH, S.M. (1990). ' Family influences on dropout behavior in one California high school', *Sociology of Education*, **63**, 283-99.

RUTTER, M. (1983). 'School effects on pupil progress: research findings and policy implications', *Child Development*, **54**, 1, 1-29.

RUTTER, M., MAUGHAN, B., MORTIMORE, P. and OUSTON, J. (1979). *Fifteen Thousand Hours: Secondary Schools and their Effects on Children*. London: Open Books.

SAUNDERS, L. (1991). The work-related curriculum: the new entitlement? Paper presented at the NFER Annual Conference, London, 6 December.

SCHMUCK, R.A. (1977). 'Peer groups as settings for learnings', *Theory and Practice*, **16**, 4, 272-9.

SCOTTISH COUNCIL FOR RESEARCH IN EDUCATION (1988). *Motivation in Education. What Role for Research?* (Forum on Educational Research in Scotland, Third Meeting, 20 November, 1987). Edinburgh: Scottish Council for Research in Education.

SHARP, A. and THOMSON, G.O.B. (1984). 'Performance in external examinations and pupils' orientations to studying,', *Educational Review*, **36**, 1, 37-51.

SKELTON, L. (1992). 'Making it too hard to figure out', *Times Educational Supplement*, 3968, 17 July, p. 22.

STOLL, L., and FINK, D. (1988). 'Educational change: an international perspective', *International Journal of Educational Management*, **2**, 3, 26-31.

STRADLING, R. (1991). Pre-vocational education and training: lessons from Europe. Paper presented at the NFER Annual Conference, London, 6 December.

SWANN REPORT. GREAT BRITAIN, DEPARTMENT OF EDUCATION AND SCIENCE. COMMITTEE OF INQUIRY INTO THE EDUCATION OF CHILDREN FROM ETHNIC MINORITY GROUPS (1985). *Education for All* (Cmnd.9453). London: HMSO.

THE GUARDIAN EDUCATION SPECIAL (1992) 'On your marks in The Guardian.' Thursday November 1992.

VARLAAM, A. and SHAW, A. (1984). 'Attitudes to school: a study of 5th year pupils.' In: HARGREAVES REPORT. GREAT BRITAIN. INNER LONDON EDUCATION AUTHORITY. COMMITTEE ON THE CURRICULUM AND ORGANISATION OF SECONDARY SCHOOLS. *Improving Secondary Schools*. London: Inner London Education Authority.

VEERMAN, P.E. (1987). 'Therapeutic tutoring and the battle against truancy in Amsterdam', *Journal of Educational Therapy*, **1**, 3, 60-72.

WEDGE, P. and PROSSER, H. (1973) *Born to Fail?* London: Arrow Books.

WEHLAGE, G.G. and RUTTER, R.A. (1986). 'Dropping out: how much do schools contribute to the problem?' *Teachers College Record*, **87**, 3, 374-92.

WEINDLING, D. (1989). 'The process of school improvement: some practical messages from research,' *School Organisation*, **9**, 1, 53-64.

WEST, A., DAVIES, J. and SCOTT, G. (1992). 'Attitudes to secondary school: parents' views over a five year period', *Research Papers in Education*, **7**, 2, 129-49.

WESTON, P. (Ed) (1990). *Assessment, Progression and Purposeful Learning in Europe. A Study for the Commission of the European Communities.* Slough: NFER.

WILLIAMS, T. and BATTEN, M. (1981). *The Quality of School Life* (ACER Research Monograph No.12). Hawthorn, Vic: Australian Council for Research in Education.

WINIARSKI-JONES, T. (1988). 'Adolscent peer groups: their formation and effects on attitudes towards education and academic performance', *Research in Education,* **40**, 51-8.

WRIGHT, J.D. and WRIGHT, S.R. (1976). 'Social class and parental values for children', *American Sociological Review,* **41**, 527-37.